MAY AYIM

Blues in Black and White

A Collection of Essays, Poetry, and Conversations

Translated and with an Introduction by
Anne V. Adams

Africa World Press, Inc.

P.O. Box 1892
Trenton, NJ 08607

P.O. Box 48
Asmara, ERITREA

Africa World Press, Inc.

P.O. Box 1892
Trenton, NJ 08607

P.O. Box 48
Asmara, ERITREA

Cover and book design: Roger Dormann

Library of Congress Cataloging-in-Publication Data

Ayim, May, 1960-1996
  [Selections. English. 2002]
  Blues in black and white: a collection of essays, poetry and conversations / by May Ayim; translated and with an introduction by Anne V. Adams.
    p. cm.
  "The translated poems presented in this collection ... are taken from Ayim's two volumes Blues in schwarz-weiss and Nachtgesang" -- Translator's introd.
  ISBN 0-86543-889-7 – ISBN 0-86543-890-0 (pbk.)
  1. Blacks--Germany--Literary collections. 2. Germany--Race relations--Literary collections. 3. Ayim, May, 1960--Translations into English. I. Adams, Anne V. II. Title.

PT2661.Y56 B58 2002
831'.914--dc21

                                    2002002720

Table of Contents

Reggae Fi May Ayim

it weard ow life wid det kyan canspyah
fi shattah di awts most fragile diziah
ow histri an byagrafi kyan plat gense yu
an dem 'angst' an dem 'anomie' gang-up pon yu

afro-german warrior woman
from hamburg via bremen
den finally
berlin

it woz in di dazzlin atmosfare
a di black radical bookfair
dat mi site yu
sweet sistah
brite-eyed like hope
like a young antelope
who couda cope

wid di daily deflowahin a di spirit
wid di evryday erowshan a di soul

two passin clouds you and I
inna di dezert a di sky
exchingin vaypah

but in di commerc a di awt
woz it fair trade in regret
in love an lauftah?

mi nevah know
mi coudn tell

mi shouda site seh

tru all di learnin
    di teachin
    rizistin
    an assistin
    di lovin
    di givin
    organizin
    an difyin

dat di kaizah a darkness
did kyapcha yu awt
dat di lass time mi si yu
would be di lass time mi si yu
dat you woz free
fallin screamin
terteen stanzahs doun
yu final poem in blood pan di groun
dat soh sudden dat soh soon
you wouda fly out
pon a wan way tickit to ghana
gaan ketch up wid you paas
mongst yu ancestaz

wi give tanks
fi di life
yu share wid wi
wi give tanks
fi di lite
yu shine pon wi
wi give tanks
fi di love
yu showah pon wi

wi give tanks
fi yu memahri

blues in black and white

over and over again
there are those who are
dismembered, sold off and distributed
those who always are, were, and shall remain the others
over and over again
the actual others declare themselves
the only real ones
over and over again
the actual others declare on us
war

it's the blues in black-and-white
1/3rd of the world
dances over
the other
2/3rds
they celebrate in white
we mourn in black
it's the blues in black-and-white
it's the blues

a reunited germany
celebrates itself in 1990
without its immigrants, refugees, jewish and black people
it celebrates in its intimate circle
it celebrates in white

but it's the blues in black-and-white
it's the blues
united germany united europe united states
celebrates 1992

4

500 years since columbus
500 years — of slavery, exploitation and genocide in the
americas
asia
and africa

1/3rd of the world unites
against the other 2/3rds
in the rhythm of racism, sexism, and anti-semitism
they want to isolate us; eradicate our history
or mystify it to the point of
irrecognition
it's the blues in black-and-white
it's the blues

but we're sure of it — we're sure
1/3rd of humanity celebrates in white
2/3rds of humanity doesn't join the party

1990

(Translation: Tina Campt; from *blues in schwarz weiss*)

Translator's Introduction

By Anne V. Adams

Fifteen years ago the path-breaking *Farbe Bekennen*[1], and its English version six years later, *Showing Our Colors*,[2] introduced Afro-Germans, the relative "new kids on the block" to the wider African Diaspora, as well as to other audiences. Subsequently other communities of the Diaspora have energetically pursued contact with, and further knowledge of, their Afro-German "sisters and brothers." May Ayim (formerly Opitz[3]), whose master's thesis provided the impetus for the *Farbe Bekennen* project, became an international voice for Afro-Germans, both as poet and as public speaker, particularly in Europe, North America and Africa. The 1994 Pan-African Festival of Theatre Arts, held in her (estranged) father's land, Ghana, afforded Ayim the opportunity to introduce Afro-Germans to a specifically Pan-African intellectual and artistic audience.

Later publications by Afro-Germans appearing in English translation since *Showing Our Colors* have expanded the range of Afro-German voices among international audiences. These include the autobiographies *Destined to Witness*, by Hans-Jürgen Massaquoi,[4] and *Invisible Woman*, by Ika Hügel-Marshall,[5] respectively. The books, in turn, have brought speaking invitations to their authors, subsequently generating further visibility for Afro-Germans outside of Germany. Research projects, conferences, doctoral dissertations and publications about Afro-Germans by U.S. scholars, generally, and by African-Americans, particularly, have been generated by these initial works. For scholars of the African Diaspora this is a previously unknown segment of the Diaspora; for German Studies

7

scholars it is a previously unacknowledged segment of the German population except as the unfortunate (or undesirable) inferior "products" of wars, which needed to be dealt with so as to minimize the effect of their presence on the society.

The present book, a collection of essays by May Ayim published posthumously, including a selection of her poetry, moves the testimony and analysis of the Afro-German experience a critical step forward in the context of pre- and post-reunified German society, on the one hand, and of an extended African Diaspora, on the other. Unique in the Diaspora because of the absence of black *enclaves* in Germany historically, the Afro-German population has forged community only within the past generation or so. This black German community, with its attendant institutions and organs, has evolved from the coming together of scattered individuals—primarily biracial native Germans but also some African, African-American and Caribbean immigrants of the past two decades—who find themselves, often isolated, but sometimes in enclaves, living in a deluded "Aryan" Germany where anyone "different" is synonymous with "foreign." It is a Germany that might grudgingly accept the label "multi-cultural" ("multi-kulti," as it is cynically colloquiaized) but *not* multi-racial. In fact, as with "black British," which, in its political connotation, embraces other peoples of color besides those of African descent, "black Germans," Ayim points out, also can embrace non-African residents of color in Germany.

So many of Ayim's observations, examples, conclusions, and cited studies resonate with nearly the exact same situations of blacks in the U.S. and Britain—where black *communities* have historically existed—for five and three centuries, respectively. For example, the assumption that all blacks can sing, dance, and/or excel at athletics; or the assertion by whites that blacks are "too sensitive" when they recognize racist remarks for what they are, even when coming from well-meaning,

"But-you know I'm not-racist!" friends; and, of course, living with the constant potential of racial violence—all of these issues discussed in Ayim's essays find their counterparts in the same forms elsewhere in the Diaspora where blacks are a minority. For example:

> Given the stereotype that blacks are supposed to be intellectually less stimulated and capable...they are expected to be above average in effort, neatness, propriety, intelligence, cleanliness and behavior.

> We as blacks place tremendous pressure upon each other: We...would like to see other blacks...represent as spokespersons and activists the interests of the black population. A black person appearing in front of the camera, for example, is expected not to "disgrace" other blacks. ... We wish to see ourselves as one, but we aren't. Some of us have managed, for example, to live in a racist environment by assimilating quite well, while others in similar circumstances have become rebellious.

These statements could well have been made by blacks of the U.S. or the U.K. How many black Americans or black Britons or black Canadians entering newly integrated schools or white-collar jobs have been told that they had to show that they were better than their white counterparts in order to be considered equally qualified? And how many times have blacks, viewing other blacks on TV, cringed when the TV personality either appeared to be "acting white" or acting like an "ignorant black"? Even though the situations described in those statements replicate experiences common to North American and British black people during the social revolution of integrating schools, workplaces, media, etc., the quoted remarks were in fact made by and about Afro-Germans, reflecting their contemporary experience. What is different, however, about the Afro-Germans' situation in time and place is that, unlike African-Americans and black Britons (and other, particularly post-colonial, black Diaspora communities), there was virtually no consciousness, hence, no articulation of their experience in German public fora before the 1980s. There was no recognition by Germans of African descent that they were a constituent minority of the German population. Before the 1980s *there was no "Afro-German."*[6]

However, since the activism of May Ayim and others, in public-speaking fora and in the printed word, the voice of Afro-Germans has extended the conscious boundaries of African Diaspora among black minority communities, in Europe and North America particularly. What May Ayim writes in the essays in this collection resonates with experiences, sensibilities, reactions, aspirations—of other quarters of the Black Diaspora.

But beyond those experiences common to the Diaspora, the situation of Afro-Germans, growing up as isolated, marginalized individuals, brings additional insights into questions of identity, psychological and social struggle. Departing from the study of the history of blacks in Germany and the narrated life-histories that furnished the contents of *Showing Our Colors*, the essays in *Blues in Black and White* bring the activist's analysis of social-scientific phenomena, touching upon economics, politics, communications, and other contemporary perspectives.

The eight essays by and conversations with May Ayim in this collection address the issues that characterized her activism and her identity as a black-German-woman. "White Stress and Black Nerves" and "Racism and Resistance in United Germany" analyze the growing up and the everyday sensibilities

and experiences of black Germans, in school and neighborhood, the job hunt or workplace, media images, etc. "We Want
Out of Our Isolation," "The Year 1990" and "The Afro-German Minority" focus on the formation of an Afro-German
identity and the resultant community and institutions among
black Germans, both preceding and following reunification in
1990. "A Letter from Muenster" and "Blacks' Rage/Whites'
Outrage" examine relations between Afro-German and other
marginalized women, on one side, and their white German
counterparts, on the other, in both individual and group
encounters. "One of the Others" recounts Ayim's trip to
Ghana in search of her family heritage. While the topic of
blacks in relation to the reunification is specific to Germany,
the material of all of the other essays substantially mirrors the
wider black Diaspora. Whether it is an account of the everyday
psychological stress of being black in a predominantly white
environment; whether it is the experiences of black and white
women's groups attempting to dialogue and collaborate; or
whether it is the articulation of blacks' need for their own institutions, organizations—"spaces"—Ayim's essays echo in
many instances those same experiences from other, longer
established communities of the black Diaspora. Her statement
on that subject captures the position of the seasoned black
activist from anywhere in the Diaspora:

> It is important that we as black people create
> spaces in which we can be among "ourselves,"
> in order to comprehend our commonalties and
> differences, to exploit them in our everyday
> lives and political work. But also, just for once
> not to be confronted with white racism, to cre-
> ate some moments of relaxation and release for
> ourselves. For the dismantling of institutional-
> ized discrimination we must constantly, but
> selectively, enter into coalitions with as many

11

marginalized groups as possible and with progressive whites...

Complementary to essays and interviews, a natural artistic
partner to those forms of May Ayim's activist voice was her
poetry. As Silke Mertins says in the biographical essay that closes the book, May felt most at home when composing verse in
her mother tongue. Manipulating the words of her language in
composing her poetry May "sharpened them to word-
weapons, to hit 'the bull's eye' with a formulation, took that
apart, put it back together anew, contorted and disfigured it or
played around with its letters..." This relationship of the
minority writer toward the formal language has also been
expressed by canonical black writers such as Aimé Cesaire and
Toni Morrison, who both have stated their intent, their need,
to transform, even contort, their respective languages, in order
to make them serve their artistic expression as black writers.
Other black writers like Maryse Condé and Audre Lorde who
did know Ayim's poetry appreciated her poetic articulation of
the black experience. Black British dub poet Linton Kwesi
Johnson, who had known May and her work through London's annual Black and Radical Book Fair, would eulogize her
in "Reggae Fi May Ayim."

The translated poems presented in this collection, which
have all appeared in publication elsewhere, are taken from
Ayim's two volumes *blues in schwarz-weiß* and *nachtgesang*.
The voice of these poems declaims the "borderless and brazen"
identity that this black-and-German woman worked out for
herself. But another side of that borderless-and-brazen persona
is the motherless/fatherless elusive identity that haunted this
German-and-African orphan. With irony and wit the poetry
directly addresses, even converses with, white compatriots,
compelling them to acknowledge her and to recognize that she
belongs there as much as they. The poetry embraces her black

12

sisters and brothers, in Germany and elsewhere, in struggle and in love; it questions the distant ties to her parentage. The poetry comments on national events as those affect minority citizens. Characteristic of poetry of the African Diaspora, May Ayim's poems are personal but transparently political, turning mother-tongue into nation-language.

Notes

1. Katharina Oguntoye, May Opitz, Dagmar Schultz eds., *Farbe Bekennen: Afro-Deutsche Frauen auf den Spuren ihrer Geschichte* (Berlin: Orlanda Frauerverlag, 1986).
2. Oguntoye, Opitz, Schultz eds., (*Farbe Bekennen) Showing Our Colors: Afro-German Women Speak Out*, A. V. Adams transl. (Amherst: UMassP 1992)
3. Opitz was the name of May Ayim's foster family. She took on her father's family name Ayim as a pen-name in 1992.
4. Hans-Jürgen Massaquoi, *Destined to Witness* (New York: William Morrow, 1999).
5. Ika Hügel-Marshall, (*Daheim Unterwegs) Invisible Woman: Growing Up Black in Germany*, Elizabeth Gaffney, transl. (NY: Continuum International Publishing Group, 2001)
6. For the most part Germans of African descent who identify as such alternate the terms *Schwarze* [blacks], *schwarze Deutsche* [black Germans], and *Afro-Deutsche* [Afro-Germans] with great fluidity, if not interchangeably. Their references are political as well as racial/ethnic. I am deploying the English terms here in the same way.

afro-german I

You're Afro-German?
...oh, I see: African and German.
An interesting mixture, huh?
You know: there are people that still think
Mulattos won't get
as far in life
as whites

I don't believe that.
I mean: given the same type of education...
You're pretty lucky you grew up *here*.
With German parents even. Think of that!

D'you want to go back some day, hm?
What? You've never been in your Dad's home
          country?
That's so sad...Listen, if you ask me:
A person's origin, see, really leaves quite a
          Mark.
Take me, I'm from Westphalia,
and I feel
that's where I belong...

Oh boy! All the misery there is in the world!
Be glad
You didn't stay in the bush.
You wouldn't be where you are today!

I mean, you're really an intelligent girl, you
          know.
If you work hard at your studies,

you can help your people in Africa, see:
      That's
What you're predestined to do,
I'm sure they'll listen to you,
while people like us –
there's such a difference in cultural levels...

What do you mean, do something here? What
      On earth would you want to do here?
Okay, okay, so it's not all sunshine and roses.
      But I think everybody should put their own
      house in order first!

1985

(Translation by Ilse Müller; from *blues in schwarz weiss*)

afro-german II

...hm, I understand.

You can thank your lucky stars you're not
       Turkish, right?
I mean: it's awful the way they pick on
       Foreigners,
do you ever run into that at all?

"..."

Well, sure, but *that's* the kind of problem I
       have, too.
I feel a person can't blame everything on the
       color of their skin, and things are never
       easy for you if you're a woman.

Take this friend of mine:
she's pretty heavy,
and does she have problems!
Compared to her, you know, you seem pretty
       laid-back.

Anyway, I feel
that blacks have kept a sort of natural
       outlook on life.

While here: everything's pretty screwed up,
       right?
I think I'd be glad if I were you.
German history isn't something one

Can really be proud of, is it.
And you're not that black anyway, you know.

1985

(Translation by Ilse Müller; from *blues in schwarz weiss*)

A Letter from Muenster

In 1984 the "First Joint Conference of Immigrant and German Women" was held in Frankfurt am Main. Tackling the question "Are we really so different?" women gathered by the thousands, among them a then-young woman coming from Muenster named May Opitz. After the conference the organizers received the following letter from her.

Dear Women of the Organizing Committee,

I am writing this summary of the weekend in Frankfurt not just for you but moreso for myself. The women's conference, as an encounter and exchange with German and foreign women, became for me personally an epiphany: many conflicts violently erupted within me that I would previously often just swallow or suppress as individualized over-sensitivity. I went to Frankfurt with fairly mixed feelings at first. I had never been to a women's event, had not really given much thought to feminism, and didn't know the exact agenda of the conference. Since I had not located any women in Muenster who were going, I got a ride through the bulletin board and left accompanied by the vague anxiety of being swallowed up in that enormous city where I had never been before. But once there in Frankfurt, I immediately found the Technical School and joined with dozens of women who were also attending the conference.

Entering, I was astonished at the large number of women! Sitting, standing, eating, talking: they were everywhere. There were hundreds of them! An indescribably colorful, comfortable atmosphere. Sleeping accommodations were assigned; there were refreshment stands. Even though I knew no one at first, I felt very secure. Making friends was easy.

The greetings in several languages and the opening statements with their differentiation and specificity impressed me. I found reflected, in each presentation, a part of my own dilemma, hope, and helplessness. And even though I had not yet read the program and was only going by the main theme, it felt right being there; it seemed that I had unconsciously been waiting a long time for a gathering like this one.

To explain this, I must tell you something about myself. I was born in Germany. My father comes from Ghana; my mother is German. There is no contact between my mother and me; I have only scant acquaintance with my father through occasional letters and a strife-ridden, two-month encounter two years ago.

Immediately after I was born I was placed in an orphanage, and after 18 months, from there into a German family as a foster child. Looking back on it I realize that this family's history was marked by mounting alienation stemming from lack of understanding, inadequate voicing of feelings, concealed and open aggression. It had the effect that, after completing high school in 1979, I initially had no communication with my foster parents and siblings for three years; and even today the occasional contacts that we do have are only very superficial.

This inner conflict between belonging and unbelonging between me and "my" foster family and me and "my" family in Africa—manifested itself for me as a contradiction between a dark skin and a German nationality. Formalities and external appearances need not and ought not have any actual significance. However, the meaning of this merely apparent disjuncture of skin color and nationality, as it affects identity formation for me, having grown up in a society where so much is made of outward difference, was unequivocally brought home to me on that weekend: My socialization was that of a "German" girl within a German milieu (in my family there was and is no contact with foreigners). I have a German name and, having also German nationality, I get to "enjoy" the privileges of being a German "national." I speak no African language, have never been in the land of my father's birth; in short, I am no foreigner. To me it's unnecessary to make an issue of my "Germanness."

However, I'm constantly asked about my origins. So when I say, "I was born and raised in Germany...," it's hardly ever accepted. What usually follows is: "But you're so 'different'-looking" or "Still, don't you want to go back to your home someday?" or "But there's no denying blood," or "Don't you think you're probably needed perhaps much more in Ghana, whereas in Germany there are so many unemployed people?!" Or I have to deal with statements like: "Well, you can be proud to have been raised in a German family"—things like that, plus having the baker's wife around the corner always using "foreigner German" with me, despite the fact that I speak to her only in grammatically correct German.

And yet I can understand her just fine, as well as the others with their well-meaning advice, their amazement, and horrified imagination, all of which offend me equally. For as a child I, too, learned the song about the ten little niggers. I, too, used to love "nigger kisses," even if I hated the word, because other kids often called me that. I, too, used to play the game "Who's afraid of the black man"; and when, the one time, my African father came to visit, I, too, wished I could run away, as the other kids did. Yes, and I, too, often without thinking, use the German language with those same racist elements that are often directed at me.

Why have I written all of this about myself and in such personal detail? Maybe because the workshop in which I participated on that weekend split into two opposing groups, immigrant women against German women. Earlier I had the feeling that I was not being accepted as an autonomous woman, especially when I was repeatedly asked "Do you consider yourself a German or an African?" This question I hear over and over from Germans and from Africans, from men and women, regardless of their level of education and nationality. I don't like being asked all the time: "Do you have a white or a black boyfriend?" I want people I meet to judge me only by the impression I make as a woman and not for my nationality or skin color.

I am not alone in wanting this, as I learned for the first time. There are so many who are insecure in their identity, as victims of racism and xenophobia, and who, through treatment as women and exotics become further hindered in developing their female capabilities and strengths. As a result I realized that I must not hold back but must speak. And that weekend I got the courage to write a paper on "Xenophobia and Racism" based on my own condition and that of so many other women.

I would like to thank you all for the congenial interaction, for every battle with you and inner conflict with myself. I look forward to many more encounters like those of this conference.

almost not at all

i never knew you at all
and, after we
saw each other
for five minutes
years ago
hardly at all

five minutes brown hair brown eyes nervous mouth
five minutes and back then nine months
forced child/motherhood
we never knew each other at all
and now, almost not at all

1985
for Ursula

(Translation by Anne V. Adams; from *blues in schwarz weiss*)

fatherseeking

when I needed you
I held the picture on the wall
to be true
the most beautiful thing I had from you
the only thing

you were
as I wished you to be
serious and smart and tender. infinitely tender.
        face to face
        your glance caught me
        serious and smart and cold. bitter cold.
        without words
                I hung the picture
                that dreamed for me
                a dream of father
                bittersweet the parting

I go and wonder

1985
for Nuwokpor

(Translation by Anne V. Adams; from *blues in schwarz weiss*)

mama

tell me mama
what was it like for you then
when you picked me up
one and a half years of age
tell me were you
happy about me

tell me and what
was it like with me on the street
white mother black child
was it terrible
and beautiful
always being in the center

tell me mama
why did you
beat me so often and so hard
just because i wet the bed
even at the age of twelve
did you really believe
i only wanted to harm you

and mama
after years of separation
we now chatter along
even though there is so much to say
the poem in my pocket
i'm silent before you
and i wish
you would ask something

(Translation by Ekpenyong Ani; from *nachtgesang*)

We want out of our isolation

May Ayim and John Amoateng-Kantara belonged to the first members of the group "Initiative of Blacks in Berlin." In 1987 they spoke with the (now defunct) magazine AWA-FINNABA. (Original reprint)

May: We are called "Initiative Schwarze in Berlin," all of us Black Germans feel this isolation and would like to meet. When I was growing up with my white foster parents, I was the only black. At school and later at university in Bavaria I was alone. Here in Berlin, I started meeting other black Germans like Nii and Martin (co-founders of the group) and the idea to organize ourselves crystallized. We advertised in the papers and invited people by word-of-mouth. About 30 people ranging between 14 and 28 years of age turned up. Amongst us are Afro-Germans (in the majority), Afro-British and even Afro-Russians.

There's another group in Frankfurt/Wiesbaden of about 20 members between 30-40 years of age. Our ideas are similar but they call themselves "Initiative Schwarze Deutsche." They exist for two years now. There are a few people in Aachen, Cologne and Stuttgart who are beginning to organize themselves.

John: The reason why people have joined our group, is for me an emotional one, this feeling to get to know other black Germans. Up to now most of us have been living in isolation. What we have lacked is a disciplined and engaged group which will bring us together. As a group we can better react to racism, protect ourselves. We need to lobby to speak out our interests, so as to check racism.

May: We are all confronted with marginalization in this society. I'm not sure if everybody would call this racism. We want to do something against it. We are tired of being alone amongst white people and having always to explain your feelings. You see, here in Germany there's no real discussion about racism. They talk about "Ausländerfeindlichkeit"[xenophobia], but seldom call it racism. With this long word they try to hide the real intensity and structures of racism. People mention that foreigners are different from the Germans. How they look, their religious/cultural practice, like the Turks. But in the situation of black Germans they can't say this. They would like to see us as a problem. These poor Afro-Germans, they are mixed. They have a problem. We have no problem with our colour, but the society creates difficulties for us.

John: There's a certain image, a wrong image society has of us. Seen in a historic view, this image was created during the time of German colonies in Africa. They saw blacks as colonial subjects. Today, the society still has these images and we are trying to correct that.

May: Last December, there was a nationwide meeting of Afro-Germans in Frankfurt. Some of the points covered by the discussion groups were: "Image of Blacks in the Mass Media," "Problems of Child Rearing amongst Afro-German Couples," "Everyday Racism in Germany," "Feeling Estranged."

I was with the group working on stereotypes of blacks in the media. This question has affected most of us. At school here, they expect a black child to excel in sports, music and dancing. These expectations are forced on the child. It's possible for one to overreact against this and have nothing to do with sports and music. Even if the black child loves Reggae music.

John: This depends also on how parents raise the child. Some parents welcomed our attempt and pledged support. Yet others are skeptical because they don't know exactly what we are doing. Afro-German couples do not have it easy. Those of us who are raised by the mother alone, miss the link to Africa. Most of the single mothers have no experience with the continent and it is impossible for them to make the child aware of its African roots.

May: I think this differs from generation to generation. Here in Berlin now one can see so many Afro-Germans. The generation before were referred to as "Besatzungskinder" (children of occupation forces) and had a stigma since people saw them as being born out of the rape by the soldiers and not born out of love.

To come back to the question of images, I think we have to find out our own history. Most of us in the group cannot imagine that there were black Germans during Fascism here. I have read about Fasia Jansen, an Afro-German woman from Dortmund, who, during the War, was forced to cook for the Jewish women in a concentration camp. Around 1700 a black student from Ghana at the University of Halle wrote his Law thesis on "The Rights of the Moors in Europe." And 200 years later the society still treats us as exotic, strange fruits. We have to inform each other, as our levels of knowledge are not the same.

John: Marcus Garvey has said: "A people without knowledge of their history is like a tree without roots."

May: Of course it is important to know more about African history, progressive black movements, about the struggle in South Africa. It is one thing to explain that blacks had great civilizations, achievements and progress. But that alone will not change the status quo. We do not as yet have the power to put our wishes across.

When as a youngster I visited Kenya, I was surprised to find African people admiring me because of being near-white. Africans get the same wrong view exported there through colonialist films and advertisements. This affects the way they look at themselves. As a child, I was somehow made to wish that I were white. The African child is made to share this wish. Children's books spreading the stereotype black and racist ideas are printed in Europe, translated and distributed to Third World countries. There's money behind this. Racism crosses borders and oceans to spread cultural domination by Europe.

calm of the storm

sometimes
the beautiful moments shine until
today and
stroked wounds whisper
pain
in gentle dreams
best
I like to see us
playing in the sandbox
stirring earth and water to mudpies
the houses we built were beautiful and
fragile
the blows
to head and bones
bolts like lightening
when we laughed at THEM and cried
our nearness grew
I loved laughing with you!

Sometimes the beautiful moment
Shines until today
I stir mudpies
And draw our faces

1985
for Holk

(Translation by Anne V. Adams; from *blues in schwarz weiss*)

sister

why do you pierce me
with your eyes
why do you want to understand everything

touch
the pain
behind my laughter

feel
the weariness
in my eyes

count
the furrows
on my forehead

examine
the scars
under my skin

why do you want to fold your cold hands
around my trembling heart

we are sisters
        you and i

we are sisters

1991
for Diane
(Translation by Ekpenyong Ani; from *blues in schwarz weiss*)

One of the Others

"How do women experience the African continent?" was the topic of the travel book Schwarzafrika der Frauen [Africa for Women], *published in 1989. May Ayim wrote her entry for the section "On My Father's Trail: Afro-German Women."*

In 1986 I spent three months in Ghana, my father's native country. Having grown up with German foster parents, I, of course, spoke not one word of Twi or any of the other indigenous languages; in fact I was glad I could communicate with some competence with my knowledge of English.

The closer my departure came, the stronger were my doubts about how well I had prepared myself for the journey. How many medicines should I take, any warm clothing, gifts, contact addresses?

I was glad to be finally standing at the airport. With all the vacillating, trying to make up my mind, I ended up taking only a minimum of everything (which I didn't regret later). The baggage scale showed eleven kilos, including youth hostel sleeping bag, mosquito net, and the one warm sweater in case it got cool. Actually, in spite of the rainy season, it was nearly always hot; even the few rain showers cooled things down for only brief periods.

For a part of the trip I had signed up with an international work camp program that collaborated with a Ghanaian organization carrying out projects dealing with rural social and economic structures. After a while I came to the conclusion that many of the projects, though initiated with good intentions, ended up at some point uncompleted. Consequently there were school buildings and farm plots started that no one bothered with anymore after the end of the work camp. Besides the scarcity of raw materials, tools and building materials, my only explanation for it is that the villagers, the actual beneficiaries of the project, had not been sufficiently included in the planning. As a result many projects went ahead in consultation with only a few insiders and supervisors and continued only as long as the sponsoring organizations sent work campers and money from outside.

Of course, the work tours in different villages provided the European campers, including myself, a unique opportunity for close contact with Ghanaians by working and living together. Likewise, many Ghanaians responded positively to meeting Europeans other than as travelers passing through and as money-spending tourists. Nevertheless we would be deceiving ourselves to claim that through our work we actually contributed to Ghana's economic and social development. All in all there is still the feeling of at least not having done any great harm, along with the memory of goodwill and of having spent a meaningful vacation rather than wasting it away.

For me the work project was not so much a priority. By no means had I gone to Ghana for the purpose of helping or seeking relaxation and a change of scenery. Of far greater importance was my desire to know the roots of my African background, to feel the life of the country where I might just as well—maybe even better—have grown up as in the FRG.

But I didn't grow up in Ghana. And even if I was able to move about the streets unnoticed and unharrassed with questions—a pleasant contrast to my everyday experience in German cities—that carefree feeling came to an end as soon as I opened my mouth to speak: a black German?! A black woman who grew up in a white family?

In fact the questions that I was asked over and over were not so very different from those in Germany. However, there was one substantive difference: Even though I was quickly perceived by many Ghanaians as a white European, and even often referred to as *White Lady*, no one ever considered not accepting me as a Ghanaian anyway. Not only that no one thought it necessary to remark that Germany was where I belonged; as a matter of fact, many thanked me for having taken the long journey to search out my African heritage and expressed their hope that I might someday remain indefinitely.

I found this friendliness to be, on the one hand, quite normal, in its straightforwardness of expression, but, at the same time, like a sort of gift, something very special. How often, in my German "homeland," am I required to cut myself off from "foreigners" in order to be competitive in the housing and job markets, that is, to have equal rights with white Germans. Basically I would have to be as "white" as possible and appear as "exotic" as necessary, to be accepted in the society where I was born and raised. Not so in Ghana. I clearly was and felt foreign, homesick, and everything that goes with it, but never did I feel rejected, unwanted, out of place.

Whenever I would have a conversation about this with people in Ghana, most of them were astonished and horrified to hear that there was discrimination against blacks in the FRG.

"But how come? You're one of them; and here, whites have it good. In fact we give them preferential treatment, because they're guests and aren't familiar with things here."

I couldn't disagree with that. During my stay I had been in many situations where whites were brought to the front of a queue at a ticket counter to be served first—hospitality, which almost made me ashamed as an observer, but which was taken for granted, if not expected, by those to whom it was offered.

No, I had no plausible explanation for the intractability of racism in the FRG. The only ones who have any justifiable grounds for hostility and prejudice are those who have been excluded and exploited for so long. There isn't much more that I can say than that racism serves to legitimate the conditions of injustice that cannot be rationally justified, hence denigrating and belittling those whose oppression constitutes the others' power.

The fact that there is so little information disseminated in Ghana about the life and situation of blacks in the FRG can probably be attributed in part to the high expectations placed on returnees. According to those expectations it must be simply wonderful, almost like paradise in Europe. How else could it be that nearly all Europeans in Ghana are rich? Even unemployed whites can afford to leave their country for several weeks or even months for a vacation in Ghana.

It is understandably the dream of many in Ghana to go to Europe for a while, to work, use the money earned to build a life in Ghana and support the family. No one believes a Ghanaian who comes for a visit and says that things are bad for them in Germany, that he or she is not in the position to send for more family members, to finance their education and living expenses in Ghana. Surely, he must have failed or has perhaps become selfish in the absence of his family, with only his own good in mind.

In that regard it bears emphasizing that often it was the whole family that made the journey abroad possible, for virtually no one can afford a ticket to Europe on the average salary.

How difficult it is to dash the expectations and the hopes attached to them, I experienced for myself on the day I visited my father's family. It was basically an unplanned, spontaneous visit, resulting from the willingness of everyone whom I told that my father was Ghanaian to help me look for my relatives. I wasn't even certain myself whether I even wanted to make contact with anyone in the family, considering that I hardly knew my father and that it had been so long since he had lived in Ghana.

So, how would his family react to me? Who among them even knew of my existence?

Finally someone offered, with no guarantee, to gather a few pieces of information about my family, since they apparently lived not far from his hometown. When I met the man two weeks later, he told me:

"I've done my homework. I learned from a co-worker that he comes from the area that your father comes from. And, would you believe, when I was questioning him, it so happens that he is an uncle of yours. I went with him right away to your grandfather's and I am now proud to report to you that your grandfather is happily expecting you. And not only are he and his family excited about your visit, but the whole village is making preparations. I told them that you would show up there next weekend."

I know I tried to smile in appreciation, while a quiet feeling of horror crept up on me. The seemingly harmless announcements had snatched all decision-making out of my hands.

"They'll surely slaughter a cow or a goat for you."

"They'll all be so happy and convince you on the spot to stay there."

"The Ewes are very skilled in sorcery; their people are known for it. They will definitely try to keep you right there. Besides, they will be very proud that you have come from Germany to visit your relatives. You'll meet so many siblings, cousins, aunts and uncles, that you'll never again have any reason to feel alone. Maybe you'll even find a husband there."

These and similar predictions, half serious, half joking, accompanied me on the way to the Volta Region. I remember that about ten years ago, at my father's request, I had sent a picture of myself to my grandfather. My brief letter and photo caused some confusion that was only resolved months later. The fact is that I had sent my grandfather one of three photos with my father and me together. So my grandfather had a picture from when I was three years old, which caused him from then on to think I was a little sister of myself. Consequently, in his reply letter he said he had heard of the big girl but not of me, the little daughter. In any case he was awaiting the day of our arrival in his home with open arms.

So, there I stood, now, before my grandfather. He was, by now, 80 years old and I, 26. As I entered his house he came toward me, just like the letter said, with outspread arms and embraced me like I was his most beloved granddaughter. What good fortune!

That day that I spent with him I got to see more relatives than I could ever have dreamed of. The oldest among them was way over a hundred years old and the mother of the deceased grandmother. I was deeply moved at becoming a member of my extended family overnight. The whole day I was occupied with greeting and being greeted.

After I had made the journey to my relatives, some of them promised in return to visit me in Germany, for which I could only be partially enthusiastic. In Ghana it would have been possible for me to stay as long as I wished with any of the people I met, and especially with the relatives, and no one would have been disturbed. In Berlin I wasn't even living legally in my apartment, and I asked myself in all seriousness what the neighbors would say and do, particularly if Ghanaian relatives were going in an out of my place for several weeks. It was already annoying just thinking about how people on the street react when someone asks them for directions. Most likely my visitors would also be confronted with the usual "straight ahead, then turn right, then left, and then after you pass the traffic light, ask again"; whereas in Ghana someone always went with me a part of the way. All of a sudden my German environment seemed so cold and uncommunicative. But I kept my thoughts to myself; I didn't know if I could have made anyone understand them anyway.

As I said my good-byes, my grandfather gave me a loving wink. Looking at me with earnest expectation, he told me not to think about Germany so much but rather about him, about Ghana, and to bring back a little of the light that the whites had taken away from Africa.

I wasn't and am still not sure what of the gleam can be brought back and what could be done with it, here or there.

between avenui and kreuzberg

we always meet
in the distance
between
avenui and kreuzberg
beneath an old
walnutmangotree

TOGBE
smiles
waiting for me
in his hands
a bowl of fufu
full to the brim

for him
i am granddaughter
MAWULI

i bring fruit
and vegetables
for dessert
i stir cottage cheese
i am happy

yes

his son too
my father is here
eating with us
one of us
listening to us
TOGBE

teaches me patience
and understanding
he worries about me
talks of ghana
about the dreams
of the ancestors of those
with second sight

he smiles
while speaking

i
answer his questions
give thoughts to him
images of berlin
i explain
"the scene"
in kreuzberg
surrounding me

we laugh a lot
          he and i

between
avenui and kreuzberg
beneath an old
walnutmangotree
in the tangled thoughts
in the distance
— in a dream—

1993
for my grandfather (†1993)
(Translation by Ekpenyong Ani; from *nachtgesang*)

distant ties

my mother's hands
are white
i know
i don't know them
my mother
the hands

my father's hands
i know
are black
i hardly know him
my father
the hands

apart
>visions
>above gray feelings of guilt
>shadow kisses
>in the darkness

apart
>memories
>cheerful her face on his forehead
>painful german
>on his lips

apart
>forgotten
>her lips his face
>ache cheerfully
>african words

apart
> before they
> lost each other
> the daughter
> apart

i know
his dark fingers
on my hand
know
her light traces
on my skin
shadow kisses on the way

distant ties
connected distances
between continents
on the road at home

i know
in moments memory
i know
in hands the horizon
alive

1992
for Sewornu and Hiavor

(Translation by Ekpenyong Ani; from *blues in schwarz weiss*)

darkness

in the beginning there was
gentle darkness and
nervous silence
then it became very noisy
very bright

grief and astonishment opened
the doors of the present
inside there was screaming
and a confusion of voices
outside it was midnight
and spring

the house was somewhere
in or at the edge of
the city
surrounded maybe
by a lawn with
flowers on it
and high above in the sky
clouds
passing each other
in a rush and leisurely

at the time

a woman a man a child
the woman very young
the man hardly older
the child just born-–crying

the man made
the woman have a child
the woman made the child
live in a home

a mo
a fa
a chi

the mother disappeared
in the darkness of time
the father came
now and then
to visit

the child stayed
alone most of the time

the first word
was just a word

MAMA

1991

(Translation by Ekpenyong Ani; from *blues in black and white*)

1990: Home/land and Unity from an Afro-German Perspective

The anthology Entfernte Verbindungen [Distant Ties], *published in 1993, from which this text is extracted, was the product of a working group consisting of women of diverse origins, who met regularly over the course of three years.*

For me, the past two years have been shaped by rapid development and changes, not only politically but also personally. I think back to the end of 1989 and going into 1990, to the bewilderment and contradictions, the fits and starts, the recollections of things suppressed, the new discoveries.

At the time I was moving as though on an unmoored boat. I was so busy trying to avoid shipwreck in all of the whirlpool of the times, that it was nearly impossible for me to take full account of the events going on around me with any nuanced understanding. In retrospect I see some pieces only in bare outline; other pieces are much clearer viewed from a distance. It seems as though the Wall between the two Germanys cast its stony shadow well in advance of its crumbling. That shadow was cast directly into the heads of those who had accepted it, enclosed and adorned themselves with it: the Wall's shadow had been cast into our East-West brains. People from the two Germanys met one another like twins who know about their common parents but had lived separated from each other since birth.

The initial euphoria erupted as the joy of reunion between two relative strangers, trying to deny the fact that their relations up to that point had been characterized by hostilities from a distance. All across the media-landscape the talk was of German-German brothers and sisters, of united and re-united, of solidarity and feelings for fellow human beings....Indeed,

even terms like home, folk, and fatherland were suddenly—
again—on the lips of many. Again making the rounds were
words that had been used only with caution or even shunned in
both German states since the Holocaust, with uninterrupted
favor only in rightwing circles. Times change, people, too. Perhaps the questions of the times only change a bit and people's
answers, hardly at all.

The early excitement of encounter crumbled with unpre-
dictable speed, and the deceitfully won unity suffocated just as
quickly under the tight artificial cloak of liberal German folksi-
ness. Of course, previously you saw the little 'one-Germany'
flags and banners waving. Germany jackets, t-shirts, and stick-
ers were everywhere. I was amazed, in November, 1989, how
rapidly and in what enormous quantities all sorts of black-red-
gold paraphernalia appeared in the stores and even at flea markets—and in demand everywhere. I could not comprehend
what was going on in the deeper recesses of people's heads and
feelings. The white, Christian-German-Collective guilt complexes had apparently dissolved overnight, thereby tearing the
present away from the past. Who were the consumers, who,
the producers, of the freedom-for-sale, and for whom and how
many was there space in the cherished new home? Who was
embracing each other in German-German reunification, and
who was embraced, pulled in, bumped out? Who, for the first
time? Who, once again? Who, all along?

Within a few moments reunification led to the birth of a
new Federal Republic in—as far as the GDR was concerned—a
not particularly new guise. The GDR was left to the side. As
the Wall fell, many rejoiced; others felt their heads spinning.

German Fa(r)ther-land...

My fatherland is Ghana, my mother tongue is German; homeland, I carry in my shoes. When the Wall fell, I felt, for a while,
the fear of being struck down. It wasn't much, not a great fear,
but more than usual.

Since 1984 I have been living and working in West Berlin
and feel more at home in this city than anywhere else. Due to
my underdeveloped sense of direction I get lost everyday in the
streets, but compared with other cities where I lived and stud-
ied before, Berlin has always been a place where I felt pretty
much at home. My skin color is not an unusual attention-grab-
ber on the streets; here I'm not praised everyday for my good
German, and, at seminars, programs, or parties, only seldom
do I find myself the only black among an indeterminate number of whites. I still have to explain myself a lot, but not constantly. I remember former times, in small West German cities,
where I often had the feeling of being under constant observation, of getting sick of constantly searching and questioning
gazes. I remember days when I would feel especially lonely or
unbearably exposed and would be on the lookout for black
people while shopping or riding the bus. In Berlin, this anony-
mous city with its international face, those recollections faded
very quickly from my memory. With the fall of the Wall and the
period following it they returned, as though out of a dusty
drawer, into my daily life.

In the days immediately following November 9, 1989, I
noticed that hardly any immigrants or black Germans were to
be seen around town, at least only rarely any dark-skinned
ones. I wondered why not many Jews were about. I ran into a
couple of Afro-Germans whom I had met in East Berlin the
previous year, and we were glad to have more chances of getting together now. Moving around alone I wanted to breathe
in a bit of the general enthusiasm, to sense the historical

moment and share my reserved joy. Reserved because I had heard about the imminent policy-tightening regarding immigrants and asylum-seekers. And further, like other black Germans and immigrants, I knew that even a German passport did not guarantee an invitation to the East-West festivities. We sensed that along with the imminent intra-German union a growing closing off from outside would ensue—an outside that would include us. Our participation in the celebration was not invited.

The new "We" in "this our country"—Chancellor Kohl's favorite expression—did not and does not have a place for everyone.

"Out, nigger, don't you have a home to go to?"

For the first time since I had been living in Berlin I now had to protect myself almost daily against undisguised insults, hostile looks and/or openly racist offenses. As in earlier times I started again, when shopping and on public transportation, to look out for dark faces. A friend of mine, holding her Afro-German daughter on her lap in the S-Bahn,* was told "We don't need your kind anymore. There are already more than enough of us!" A ten-year-old African boy was thrown out of a crowded U-Bahn train to make room for a white German.

Those were incidents in West Berlin in November, 1989, and since 1990 reports of racially motivated attacks primarily on black people have increased, mostly in the eastern part of Germany. Reports like those were at first known only in circles of immigrants and black Germans, the official media reporters hardly taking notice of the violent assaults. I began the year 1990 with a poem:

"borderless and brazen: a poem against the German "u-not-y."

i will be african

* S-Bahn: elevated train

even if you want me to be german
and i will be german
even if my blackness does not suit you
i will go
yet another step further
to the farthest edge
where my sisters – where my brothers stand
where
o u r
FREEDOM
begins
i will go
yet another step further and another step and
will return
when i want
if i want
and remain
borderless and brazen

1990
for Jaqueline and Katharina

(Translation by May Ayim)

As an outgrowth of the "Black History Month" series of pro-grams on topics of black history, culture, and politics, initiated by a black activist group in Berlin, February, 1990, a task force was formed of black groups and individuals, which, among other things, published a first documentation of racist attacks in Berlin and the surrounding area.[1]

Around the same time I completed my training as a speech therapist. I remember not only the jittery exam time with sleepless nights and problems in my love-life, but also the meetings of black political groups at which for the first time we discussed measures for protecting our organizations and our individual persons from racist attacks. Between the two Germanys contacts among black groups and those concerned with immigrant politics intensified, leading to common actions and social gatherings. I was angry and disappointed that the liberation of Mandela received hardly any attention in the German media at that time. For the first time I came to appreciate the invention of cable TV, because I saw at least that not the entire European world was engaged in contemplating its navel.

At demonstrations against the tightening of immigration and asylum law early in the year, white German representation was scarce. The *TAZ*, on April 2, 1990, reported: "German Leftists Absent at Mass Demonstration Protesting Law on Foreigners. Too Foreign?"

I began to get angry over the East-West celebrations and programs that did not incorporate North-South dialog. In the women's movement, too, German-German matters were discussed and celebrated, as though Germany were exclusively white and the center of the world. Conferences and seminars were held, with travel support for women from the GDR, without also considering asylum-seekers, who, whether in East or West Germany, have to squeeze out a minimal existence. This modus operandi was in keeping with the after-thought, half-hearted show of solidarity staged at the governmental level by the "Better Westerners" for the "Poor Easterners."

Thinking back I recall an ad in the movies promoted by the Berlin Senate: East German workers on a construction site in West Germany. A voice off-screen announced that it was GDR citizens who were taking the underpaid jobs and those unattractive to West Germans. The commentator was exhorting the audience, in a manner both urgent and friendly, to graciously receive "the people" who have come "to us" in the recent weeks and months. Why is it that only white German men are shown, if they were talking about feelings for fellow human beings between women and men from both Germanys? I wholly support a call to solidarity but not one that is silent on the fact that the least attractive and worst-paid jobs go to migrant workers from other European and non-European countries. Where is the call to solidarity with those who, in the tide of German-German embrace, are in greatest danger of no longer finding work and housing possibilities and of losing their jobs and training posts? For asylum seekers there were no embracing gestures of support with words of goodwill and discount tickets. On the contrary, the law on temporary or permanent residence especially for people from predominantly poor non-European countries was drastically tightened by means of new legal requirements. Further, as racist violence in the streets was increasing, white citizens and politicians from East and West, until the end of 1990, stood by doing nothing. And also, the "receptivity" and "hospitality" toward white GDR citizens seemed dishonest to me in the face of the attitude toward so-called foreign compatriots, who long before now, had been constantly reminded that the "boat" is full.

Biologist Irenäus Eibl-Dibesfeld, for example, published an article in 1981 with the title "Dangers of Mass Immigration," in which he said:

> *We should have no delusions: with every immi-*
> *grant allowed in, we cede ground; and we have*
> *to tell the people like it is, for the contexts of large-*
> *scale biological integration are just as unclear to*
> *them as the possible consequences.*[2]

A clear indication of this is that only certain groups of immigrants are categorically perceived and marginalized as "foreigners," just as black Germans cannot be "real Germans."

A blond, blue-eyed woman told me that white Germans have trouble believing that she comes from Brazil. She would often be asked, "But don't your ancestors come from Germany?" In Brazil, she said, no one had ever doubted her Brazilian origins and her Brazilian nationality. Only in Germany had she begun to reflect on and research her family history. She found out that a long deceased great-grandfather had actually emigrated from Germany to Brazil. Today, whenever she introduces that bit of information into the "Where-are-you-from-conversation," the reaction is not infrequently: "Oh, that's wonderful that your ancestors are from Germany. How do you feel being in your homeland for the first time?" Black Germans have different experiences in this country.

The New German "We": An inclusive and exclusive space?

Franz Beckenbauer commented, as coach of the German soccer team, on his team's victory in the World Championship in the summer of 1990: "For years we've been unbeatable. I'm sorry for the rest of the world, but that's how it is."[3] The disturbing vision of a we-are-again-somebody Germany took on increasingly real form over the course of 1990, with the growing popularity of racist pronouncements and behaviors. Likewise, the German "we" that had been touted remained split into two different halves. The historic moment which yielded so much counterfeit rhetoric of "revolution" could have been, in both parts of Germany, a moment of critical self-reflection and mutual stimulation for change. Already at the time the Wall fell it was clear that no one was prepared to criticize and reform the FRG as rigorously as was being urged for the GDR. In government circles attention was focused first and foremost on implementing political and economic interests, and so hardly guided by humanitarian ideals.

Hans-Joachim Maaz, a psychotherapist from Halle, is one of those who posed the question in 1990:

> *Where are the honest politicians of the West, to warn and inform us about the failures and problems in our own system, and not just smugly offer us their "superiority"? Where are the serious reflections about what needs to change in the FGR, so that a unified Germany becomes an opportunity and not a new danger for Europe?*[4]

Since then, two years after the fall of the Wall, the face of the former GDR is no longer recognizable. Textbooks, laws, institutional structures, etc. were either brought into line with those of the former GFR or done away with. Flashing billboards everywhere are a clear indication that capitalism has taken a foothold in even the tiniest village of the five new federal states, and the "Trabis," already a rarity now, seem like relics from the distant past. Considering its total removal, the entire Wall story is now hard even to imagine. The number of jobless, especially women, is climbing at a staggering rate. The re-naming of streets and the removal of certain monuments are among the signs pointing out the new view of the past and the next step into the future as drafted by those in power. What will we remember? What have we already forgotten? I notice that in the renaming of streets in the new states, often names of resistance fighters are replaced by names of flowers. Hence, "Liselotte Herrmann Street" in Erfurt has been recently renamed "Medlar Street." The re-naming of East Berlin's U-Bahn station "Thälmann Street" to "Moor Street" is a sure sign that racist language and associated thinking are tolerated and carried on even in the highest white ranks of the new republic. This is evident as well in the still unchallenged retention of street names and monuments in the western part of Germany that glorify colonialists and degrade the colonized.

The silence and denial of racism even on the part of "progressive" leftists and among women's-movement women, though unsettling and shocking to me in 1990, hardly surprised me anyway. Undeniably, discussions on the subject of a "multi-cultural FRG" have been on the increase since the mid-'80s. But only in exceptional cases have they effected a change in anyone's actual day-to-day political associations, so that a continuous, egalitarian collaboration with immigrants and black Germans became indispensable and taken for granted, and confronting racism became a constant commitment. The "Second Women's Shelter" in Berlin and Orlanda Women's Press are among the few independent women's projects that have long been committed to quotas for immigrants and black women in their hiring.[5]

Racism is still seen by many white Germans as an exceptional instance and special subject. Hence, immigrants, black Germans, and Jewish people are often only considered and included within the context of special programs, as, for example, "Immigrant Neighbors Week," or a conference on "Migration and Population Policy." This is one facet of unconscious and subtle in- and exclusion. A pertinent comment from Klaus F. Geiger in November, 1989:

> *The reporter is standing on the Kurfuersten-damm, surrounded by people celebrating the fall of the Wall. He interviews first two or three people from East Berlin, then looks for West Berliners as interviewees. Behind him are standing four or five Turks caught up in the festivities, young men, between 18 and 20 years of age, shifting from one foot to the other, looking expectantly into the camera, making themselves*

> *available but not being pushy. The reporter turns
> in a circle, seeing no one that he would call a
> West Berliner, cuts off his search and turns it
> over to the studio. For today it's about the reuni-
> fication of two German territories, about the
> reunification of two peoples, who are German
> citizens by law. Had the subject of the broadcast
> been worded "Problems of Foreigners," these
> young Turkish Berliners would also have been
> appropriate interviewees—along with a lot of
> German experts.*[6]

Not until the election in the second half of 1990 did the voices of immigrants, black Germans and the Jewish community begin to be heard. At that time conferences and public events on the subject of "Racism" were multiplying, but organized in large part and sometimes exclusively by white Germans. Such was the case, for example, with the conference "Exclusion and Tolerance," held in Eindhoven in November, 1990. Even though black as well as white women scholars from the Netherlands and the Federal Republic gave papers and seminars on the subject, black women were not involved in the conceptualization and execution of the conference. Hence, for the preparations of the next conference the composition of the organizing team was revised. Fortunately, from a few other such events as well, not only were painful wounds left over but also equally fruitful initiatives for real collaboration between black and white women came out of them.

In a society marked by racism and other oppressive mechanisms the real or potential victims in each case are not at the same time the better people. Sometimes I observe, in political black-white situations, that black women or men are given unlimited time to speak, regardless of whether their intervention is useful. Preferential treatment is appropriate and necessary and an important requirement when it's a matter of allocating jobs. But that can't mean "fool's freedom." If we want to work together and regard each other as allies—and that's my assumption—then we have to take each other seriously with the courage to express and take criticism. That goes equally for blacks and whites interacting with and among one another. A particular mark of East-West encounters among whites was and still is the fact that dialog often doesn't happen unless the women and men in the new states come to sit at the discussion table on the western side of Germany. Black Germans and immigrants in the former FRG are also only now beginning to understand that it's not dialog unless their groups in East and West approach each other with equal initiative.

I am becoming increasingly conscious of how much I have been marked by certain experiences in this society and on what points I wish to eradicate or retain those marks. Often, recalling childhood dreams and experiences, I let the adults' comments pass in review, looking for meaningful messages. I dig around for repressed images and warnings. In writing this text I suddenly encountered my grandmother, who died in 1990—actually, my foster mother's mother. I saw her in her cozy kitchen and heard as she spoke with my "brother" and me. We loved her, and she always had a few sweets for us in her cabinet drawer. Now, as I saw her before me, at that moment she was annoyed by the noise we kids were making and called out in a half-joking voice: "It sounds like the Jews' school in here!" Not until later did I flinch, understanding the meaning of her words, when Granny would bend down to the youngest grandchildren with that same saying. And racist expressions came out now and then in our house, seldom consciously nor with evil intent. No one meant to be anti-Semitic or racist. Everyone abhorred the atrocities of the National Socialist past; and, after all, it wasn't just by chance that I had landed as the only black child in this white foster family. Nobody there could be prejudiced, right? Racism and anti-Semitism were some of the undesirable ingredients of the upbringing that I experienced. I am conscious of it and I won't let it go until I have rooted it out and dismantled it from myself.

Now it's 1992, the European Union is being concluded and in a few weeks the anniversary of German reunification will be celebrated. Daily—just as in summer and fall of last year and the year before last—we learn of new racist and anti-Semitic assaults, of arson against refugee quarters and of mob attacks in East and West Germany. In many places eager bystanders applaud openly or secretly, and politicians appear very concerned for the country's image, but very little for the real and potential victims of the attacks. Interior Secretary Rudolf Seiters had this to say about the escalating violence:

> *It is certainly the consensus that this is a phenomenon that damages Germany's image in the world and which could lead to the distortion and erosion of the reputation of a Germany hospitable to foreigners, which we must preserve at all costs.[7]*

Chancellor Kohl, in his address of August 27, 1992, urged: "The abuse of the right to asylum must finally be resolved. That also includes amending the constitution, which, however, will not solve the problem alone but is a major step toward stemming the abuse of asylum."[8] Recent weeks have witnessed more discussion of marginalized youth who are currently the primary perpetrators of neo-Nazi attacks. Discussions about the causes of refugee movements are not taking place, nor about measures that could end hunger, war and environmental destruction in poor countries and those which are kept dependent on Europe. An immediate and severe revision to the asylum law portends serious consequences; but even for the asylum seekers who are allowed to stay, the Federal Republic will, in the foreseeable future, not be a place to freely call "home." The same goes for immigrants, black Germans and Jewish people who have been living here all along.

The open violence in the streets resonates with the words of leading politicians and is, to some extent, their practical application. But I am convinced that we—and I am referring to all people in this country who do not tolerate racism and anti-Semitism—are desirous of and capable of coalitions. There are examples that we can follow or adapt. This is how the "Initiative of Black Germans," which was formed from a small group of Afro-Germans in the mid-80s, now has working and networking groups in a number of cities in the Federal Republic. Organizations of immigrants, black Europeans and Jews have joined in to link up their groups and activities across national boundaries. The "Intercultural Summer Institute for Black Women's Studies" has been held since 1987, with black participants from all continents.

In 1991 the hosts were black German women, and the several week-long seminars were held in Bielefeld, Frankfurt/M, and Berlin. The second conference by and for immigrant, black German, Jewish and women living in exile, which took place in Berlin in the same year, was, above all, an example of support of white Christian secularized women. Excluded as participants, they nevertheless contributed in large numbers through transportation assistance, childcare, providing overnight accommodations. Through their donations they made a critical contribution to the running of the conference. One thing is certain: The global and national structures of dependence as well as the power relations within our personal relationships are unsettling and destructive, but not static. We can bring about change!

Notes

1. Black Unity Committee (ed.), *Dokumentation: Rassistische Überfälle in Berlin und Umgebung* (January-September 1990), Berlin 1990
2. Irenäus Eibl-Eibesfeldt, "Gefahren der Masseneinwanderung," in: *Lutherische Monatshefte*, no. 1, 1981, p. 34.
3. Quoted from Norbert Seitz, "Wir sind halt doch das Volk," in: Arthur Heinrich and Klaus Neumann (eds.), *Alles Banane. Ausblicke auf das endgültige Deutschland*
4. Hans-Joachim Maaz, *Der Gefühlsstau Ein Psychogramm der DDR*, Berlin 1990, p. 182.
5. See the contribution by Dagmar Schultz in *Entfernte Verbindungen: Rassismus, Antisemitismus, Klassenunterdrückung*, Berlin 1993.
6. Klaus F. Geiger, "Nationalistische und postnationalistische Diskurse im Verteilungskampf der Bundesrepublik Deutschland," in: Institut für Migrations- und Rassismusforschung (ed.), *Rassismus und Migration in Europa*, Hamburg, Berlin 1992, p. 273.
7. Quoted from Dietrich Leder, "Medientagebuch," in: *Freitag*, 4 September 1992, no. 37.
8. Quoted from Tissy Bruns and Klaus-Peter Klingelschmitt: "Kein Wort der Scham in Bonner Kabinett" in *die tageszeitung* 28 August 1992.

no more rotten gray—for a colorful republic
talk – talk – show for the blah – blah – struggle

on special occasions
and for special events
but especially
shortly before
and shortly after elections
we're in demand again
we're taken notice of again
we're suddenly addressed
we're finally included
we suddenly seem indispensable
we are even
flown over
on your invitation of course
as the "dear alien citizens"
naturally without civil rights
as migrants
from the countries of the world
as experts in matters of racism
as the ones "afflicted"

together with activists and politicians
celebrities and the socially committed
we discuss analyze debate
about
demands protest actions appeals
in discussions hearings talk-shows
on a panel in a forum or plenum

and then—what next

the demands
are neatly
listed
the lists
are neatly
filed
and surely
and reliably
forwarded
to the right places
with the truly
responsible people

and then--what next

the show is over
we all go home

the socially committed feel relieved—partly
the afflicted feel they've been taken for a ride—totally

the "dear alien citizens"
still without civil rights of course
once again turn into the "spics," "pakis" or "chinks" from next
door
the black or however
hyphenated germans
change back into the "negroes"
from really far away
once again we are those
the whitewashers of history
already over-looked yesterday
or dis-covered
described defined instructed

in broken g/er/man
on the street
or in highly abstract studies
in a v-e-r-y s-c-i-e-n-t-i-f-i-c language
we are patiently told over and over
which way to go
why
INTEGRATION
is written in capitals
why and how
we are oppressed
why and how and when
we must liberate ourselves
why and how and when and where and most important

that doesn't take many words
nor lots of space
no
not really

the leftist alternative daily paper—so-called
for example only needs about two pages for international news
compared to about seven pages for german-german affairs
the so-called yellow press
quote: "germany in liberty that is our mission"
does it even quicker
shorter
more to the point
more capturing
the
north-south-monologue

that doesn't take many words
no, not really

that's why they hardly ever ask us
there's no space anyway
whereas we're still indispensable of course
at least on special occasions
or for special events
but certainly
shortly before the next elections
they will remember us again
we'll definitely have to be a part of it
we'll be allowed to proclaim our distress
must in fact do so
should in fact
put our demands into words
and really blast the trumpet
or at least sing a song
no more rotten gray—for a colorful republic

but
the "dear alien citizens"
although or because
still without civil rights
dress up for their own celebrations
and also the black
or however hyphenated germans
no longer come because they've been invited
but only
when they want to
they're gradually getting cheeky
bad luck
luckily!

1990
for Tina, Gülsen, Yara and Nita
(Translation by Ekpenyong Ani; from *blues in schwarz weiss*)

Blacks' Rage/Whites' Outrage

At the "First Lesbian Feminist Summer Institute," held at the Lutheran Academy of Loccum, May Ayim gave the talk "The Year 1990: Home and Unity from an Afro-German Perspective." A discussion with white participants followed.

May: Before the elections, toward the end of 1990, there were many multicultural, antiracism programs, which took the place of the East-West celebrations of the first half of the year, celebrations that included virtually no reference to immigrants and black Germans. When asked to do a cultural piece for one of the election events with the motto "Talk Show for a Colorful Republic," I wrote a poem with the title "No More Rotten Gray—For a Colorful Republic. Talk-talk-show for the blah-blah Struggle." The poem articulates how the so-called affected groups are acknowledged and given consideration just for certain occasions and special events, only to be dismissed and forgotten soon afterward.

What were the reactions to the poem?

May: The organizers were dumbfounded and somewhat offended; the moderator managed to thank me right off for the "exotic contribution." So she, at least, had not understood a thing. The ensuing discussion, in which I did not participate, did proceed, unfortunately, exactly as was described in the poem: The "affected group" was only invited to talk about "their problems." They were not taken seriously as conversation partners nor as personalities with multiple interests and areas of expertise.

My poem was subsequently printed in the *TAZ* (newspa-

64

per). Ironically it was done up with pictures from North American reservations for "exotic" reader appeal.

How is the interaction among lesbian and heterosexual Afro-Germans?

May: Within the movement of black German women the lesbians have been and continue to be the more active and the ones who, in my opinion, are more likely to risk taking radical positions. Perhaps, being affected to a greater degree by multiple experiences of discrimination, they feel more compelled to take a clear and consequential position.

What about conflicts between lesbian and straight Afro-Germans, as so often exist in the white women's movement?

May: So far I haven't observed such conflicts between black lesbian and straight women. I wouldn't say that there are none. But I think, rather, that so far Afro-German women have been forced to struggle collectively against racism in society, racism of white straight and lesbian women, and sexism of white and black men. If resistance on so many fronts were not necessary, then most likely the question of that relationship would arise anew.

The film "Schwarze Frauen bekennen Farbe [Black Women Showing Their Colors]," shown over ARD early in 1992, gave the impression that racial violence is greater in the East than in the West. What has been your experience in the ISD (Initiative of Black Germans)?

May: Originally the director Christel Priemer wanted to do a film that focused only on open racial violence. For that purpose she especially sought out women in the former GDR, since she had already made two or three films about Afro-Germans in western Germany. In the end, as with all her films about black Germans, including this one, she determined the perspectives and topics even when the black women spoke in their own words. This comes through particularly in the titles of her first films, "A Little Black, A Little White, Or What It Means to be a German Negro" (1984) and "Germans Are White, Negroes Can't Be Germans" (1986).

At the time her reaction to my criticism of the titles was that the public has to be provoked. But that's not even provocation; in fact that says exactly what people generally think about blacks. I believe it is increasingly important to put positive messages out front with such projects and not serve up the negative ("niggertive") stereotypes over and over.

To asses racism in East Germany as worse than in West Germany, is, I think, dangerous and wrong. In the final analysis the fascist groups work together at all levels and in every respect. Who is behind which action is often impossible to tell and definitely not to be described by East-West categories. More interesting is the question why those groups work together so effectively, while the anti-racist movement, though numerically stronger and with greater forces, can't achieve that. Where are the broad-based and committed actions of the women's movement in all of this?

The 1991 film started out with a black woman singer living in Hamburg. Once again an example of the cliché...

May: ...in the sense that all blacks can sing, dance, and/or excel in sports, yes. On the other hand, these areas are not considered accomplishments or professions with blacks, but are counted, or to be more exact, discounted as natural talent. For black artists it is especially difficult to move outside the accepted stereotype.

Why weren't the last names of the interviewees used in the 1991 film? Doesn't that degrade black women? Or was it done to protect them?

May: An interesting question. However, I don't know what agreements and intentions were behind that decision and whether those matters had been discussed with the subjects. As a rule, one has to be careful in publicizing names, because the people in question might otherwise wind up getting all kinds of calls and letters.

How does your group see themselves in relation to coalition partners? Do you seek coalitions?

May: There is no large, strong black community for Afro-Germans to retreat to. But that's not the goal, either. First of all, it's important to have a space where Afro-Germans can interact among themselves without interference from white Germans. Of course, being "among ourselves" is not always a bed of roses, but we have big and small differences of opinion, social- and class-differences, and, east-west differences, as well. The closer the personal or political friendship, the more painful it usually is to withstand power struggles and conflicts.

Both before and after "Reunification" white women and the Left only reacted. Finally white women spoke up but without bringing in black and immigrant women.

May: It looks that way to me, too, although there are more and more white women who are seriously facing up to their privilege and power, even though the majority still do not make this step. The more terrible things that happen, the greater the apathy becomes. The fact that white women's projects now finally include considerations of employment quotas for migrants and black women is a clear sign that all the arguments between black and white women have resulted in more than just aggression and resistance.

I am not one to praise to high heaven each little success, but it is important that we recognize our successes and encourage ourselves to go on. It is important that we not only criticize ourselves—no matter how constructively—but that we also praise ourselves and approach such serious subjects with less rancor. In particular we call on white women to take seriously black women's rage and bear it. It's unfair to expect us always to be constructive and open to dialog, after we've had no place in your ranks, no voice, and been made invisible, for the most part. Up until recently Afro-Germans didn't even have a positive term to call themselves. Who would voluntarily name herself "mixed-blood?" And the word "mulatto" originally comes from Portuguese, meaning "mule." Black women's rage must also be white women's outrage, because we've all been duped and manipulated by lies, half truths, and myths.

Often I wish I could leave Germany, but, on the other hand, it is also important to struggle here and change things.

May: I make a big distinction between those who move in and out and those who must leave and flee. From the time I was a child I've been made to understand that I have no right to be here and to stay here. At some time in my life I got to the point where I was constantly pre-occupied with the thought of where I could go. That happens to many black Germans, because the question "Where are you from? When are you going?" is always assaulting us. More than once have I heard, in looking for a job, that my African appearance might frighten or unsettle clients; in other words, bad for business.
In the meantime a few of my black friends have left Germany, several after attacks of violence or from fear. It could happen

that one day, maybe not too far off, I'll have to leave; but for the time being, I'm here.

What role does Christian socialization play for Afro-Germans?

May: By and large, Christianity definitely has a great influence in the socialization of Afro-Germans who grow up here. My first part in a play, in second grade, was the role of the devil. For all the pupils and the teacher and for me, of course, as well, it was obvious that there was no way I could play the role of the angel. Who's ever seen a black angel? In a religion class of the 50s one of my Afro-German friends was told that the reason the "moor" Balthasar had white palms and soles was that he had touched the holy ground with his feet and the Christchild with his hands.

Do you find it a contradiction that we are meeting here at the summer institute among white lesbians only and have invited you?

May: I think it's important that blacks and whites meet as it works in their own contexts in order to bring about communication with each other. However, I'm not willing to participate in every dialog. Particularly when from the outset it can only end in an exchange of blows or in a one-sided interrogation. And under no circumstances would I, for example, sit down at the table with right-wing radicals or declared sexists. I'll leave them to ex-fascists and pro-feminist men, thank you.

Many of us are theologians. We are searching for liberating traditions in Christianity. Can Christianity, in your opinion, have any relationship to liberation?

May: In my view any religion can be liberating and used for oppressive purposes as well. For me personally, Christianity provided many of the building blocks from which I have formed my own humanitarian world view. The reason that I bring up the negative messages, though, is that I only became conscious of them much later and am still having to work through them. On my first visit to Ghana I was stunned to see that Christianity was white there, too, and Eurocentric (for example, there are no black angels there, either). The collusion of mission work and colonization has strong negative effects up to today. The dominance of Christianity is worldwide. Everyone knows Jesus, everyone has to know Jesus. One of my friends told me about his German course, where, during the subject of Christmas, a Chinese asked: "Jesus, who was that?" and proved the opposite.

arrogant question

jesus
who was that, please
a chinese woman asked
surprised in a german lesson

some of them laughed
politely the others
loudly
all of them

baffled

about themselves

1992
for Achim and Werner

(Translation by Dagmar Schultz; from *blues in schwarz weiss*)

invitation

it's best you act
totally totally normal
don't ever say negress
that would be a catastrophe
of course she knows potatoes
no you needn't fry them
it's fine if you cook them
her skin is black
her hair is kinky
: welcome home

(Translation by Ekpenyong Ani; from *nachtgesang*)

White Stress/Black Nerves
Stress Factor Racism

In 1995 May Ayim wrote this article for the self-help book
Getting Rid of Stress, *which provides an overview of her research
of recent years.*

Racism is often a direct—more often, subtle—stress factor for
people of African descent. In both the old and new German
states, discrimination and violence against migrants and blacks
have recently become such obvious features of everyday life that
they can no longer be overlooked. Violent clashes are indeed
only the tip of the iceberg; no less dangerous and deeply rooted
are the subtle forms of contempt and marginalization.

Racism: A Stress Factor With a History

Discrimination and prejudice based on skin color have a long
tradition that dates back, in German society, to the pre-colo-
nial era. From as far back as the Middle Ages stereotypical
images of people of African descent can be found; at that time
they were almost exclusively based in religious stereotypes.
Western Christian color symbolism connected black to evil,
the undesirable, and the illicit. White, by contrast, symbolizes
up to today the good, the pure, the immaculate. In fact, the
early Christians considered dark-skinned people as the earthly
likeness of the devil.[1] During the Age of Enlightenment myths
and prejudices against black people took on a pseudo-scientif-
ic underpinning and soon enjoyed widespread dissemination.
Race theorists developed a human profile in which cultural and
social differences were posited, valued, and sanctioned as natural phenomena. Peoples and cultures were placed and classified

in relationship to white European culture: as "peoples of nature," considered, in comparison to Europe as "underdeveloped," "primitive," "uncivilized," "backward."

It is important to have a clear picture of the historical roots of racist thinking and behavior, for advertising, everyday speech, cartoons, and the entire modern entertainment industry make use of a comprehensive repertoire of stereotypes and ascriptions that goes back to the time of colonial conquest. The media, too, transmit a mindset of superiority or inferiority, as the case may be, with regard to the relations between "first" and "third" world: In terms of the values of the high-output industrialized societies the norms for development and progress are almost entirely quantifiable consumer goods or the statistical per capita income. Thus, they restrict themselves to techno-economic income indices. It would be equally conceivable to consider a people particularly "developed" and "civilized" who demonstrate a high degree of tranquility and harmoniousness in human relations, and, with relation to the natural environment, a special capacity to resolve conflict in the interests of all concerned. That none of these values is a measure of the status of a society and its socio-cultural manifestations is a sign of a world characterized by military build-up, increasing environmental antagonism and a growing measure of psychic illness.

The clichéd image of Africa as a continent of hunger or of "cannibals" and "primitive natives" is a humiliating burden for black people. According to the Nigerian E.M.:

> The incessant questions have become so bothersome to me that I now avoid contact with people. They're always asking me what kinds of houses "we" have, what "we" eat, how "we" live, etc. So often I notice that what lies behind this persistent questioning is not simply ignorance and the

resultant curiosity but that those asking the ques-
tions already have an established picture of
Africa, which they want to have confirmed. They
don't ask "Do you people live in mud huts and go
around naked?" but "Do you people live in prop-
erly constructed houses, what kinds of clothing do
you people wear?"2

Blacks live under the pressure of having always to vindicate themselves to whites as being "progressive" and "intelligent." What's more, they are confronted with terms and everyday popular expressions that degrade blackness as ugly, inferior, and undesirable: "riding black,"* "blacken,"+ "passing someone the black card,"∞ "seeing black"#—these are only a few examples of generally unconscious expressions, grounded in a long tradition of "black-white imagery, which affect dark-skinned people.

Even many seemingly objective references and the contents of schoolbooks, instruction and teaching materials are riddled with myths and prejudices that came into existence as long ago as the last century or earlier.

Stress Factor: Marginalization in All Its Forms

Not until the final phase of my education, when I started my own research on the history of blacks in Germany, did I become aware that that history had not begun only after World War II. To my amazement and outrage I had never heard before then that, during the the Weimar Republic and National Socialism, black people—and in significant numbers—had

---

* Riding public transportation without a ticket.
+ Blacken, as in "blacken one's reputation."
∞ Passing the buck
being blinded

fallen victim to discrimination, racist persecution, expulsion, and murder. An important part of German history had been kept from me and other schoolmates. While, from the perspective of my white schoolmates, this may have been of no consequence, for me and other Afro-Germans it meant that our self-knowledge could not come from any black models, symbols of identity, or historical roots. In the anthology *Showing Our Colors* two sisters, Doris Reiprich and Erika Ul Kuo Ngambi tell about themselves. In the Germany of the 1930s and 1940s they were exposed to constant racism on account of their skin color, and they survived a time in which their lives counted as worthless. Erika Ul Kuo Ngambi reports about her school days after 1933:

> *I had to take part in the course on "Race" and had to listen to statements like "God made all whites and Blacks, half-breeds come from the devil" or: "Half-breeds can only inherit the bad characteristics of both races."*[3]

During the Nazi period many blacks, including the two sisters, survived, because they played roles as actors and extras in colonial films. This is how they managed to endure the enormous stress brought on by racist persecution.

Black-White stress in the day-to-day life of the child

An Afro-German woman who grew up in the 1950s was taught during religion class that blacks had white soles and palms because one of the Three Magi, the "moor" Balthasar, had touched holy ground with his feet and the Christchild with his hands. I myself, as the only black child in my elementary school class' first play, was assigned the role of the devil, and a girl with long blond hair and blue eyes played opposite me as the angel. I must have been seven years old, then, and, just like my white schoolmates, assumed this basis for assigning the roles to be quite natural. For, had anyone ever seen a black angel and a white devil? Even though religious instruction, especially, in the regular schools always emphasizes that all people were created by God, nevertheless, black people are virtually never depicted and hardly ever appear in stories. When black people do show up as protagonists in books and films, they have secondary roles, performing subordinate functions.

Basically, one observes that, wherever black characters from so-called Third-World countries are actors, they are almost never fellow-citizens in Germany, but almost without exception live in other countries or continents and are presented in contrast to European life situations.

Something else I have noticed is that, in children's and young people's books, drawings of people of African descent often depict them with stereotyped facial and body forms and are associated with "wild" and "uncivilized," with the result that white children are always motivated to help "those poor people." This is the message of *Ich und Du* [Me and You] a children's book by Monika Penders and Mavis Smith, and whose publicity material from the publisher says:

> *A lively, stimulating book, in which the world of a child in civilized Europe is compared to that of a child in Africa. Even for six-year-olds a child's understanding of the necessity for humanitarian aid is engendered.*[4]

The comparison referred to is confined to material comparisons and can be reduced to the simple formula: "Here we have everything, there they have nothing." The book belongs to the selected children's books of the Peter Hammer publishing company and came out in the series *Guck mal übern Teller-rand* [Peek over the Rim]. It omits the point that people might learn from each other precisely on the basis of their differences. Indirectly and unintentionally it conveys to black children a feeling of inferiority and to white children a consciousness of living in the best of all possible worlds, of being on the giving end and of being role models. For black children this is all the more painful and devastating because they seldom have any access to black parents, grandparents, uncles and aunts, who by their very existence could contradict or counteract this image. Afro-Germans grow up, for the most part, with primarily white people to relate to; those who are brought up in orphanages or in adoptive or foster families grow up entirely around whites. Their first encounters with black people take place in the realm of children's and youth books, which determines not only their image of African women and men but also their self-awareness. Typically this happens in passing: Like other little girls of my age I loved playing "Pipi Longstocking," whose white father reigns as "negro king" in "Takatukaland"; feared the black boogeyman, who adults claimed lived behind the cellar door; believed that with every lie my soul became a little blacker. And by kindergarten I had come to realize that with my color I was exactly like those people in adventure stories and games who were always to be patronized, pitied, fought, or even extermi-nated. Black people, those were servants, slaves, and cannibals, thus placed on an even lower rung than the so-called red-skinned Indians, who, in TV films and comic books also under-stood only baby-talk German. The regular set-up when we played Africa in my childhood was usually in the "jungle," and as a black person I didn't have to do much more than run up behind white characters and obediently respond to their com-mands and orders: "Yes, Massa, right away. Massa" formed a standard incantation in the black-white dialog. There were rarely female heroes, not to mention black heroines; but definitely black monsters who produced many little monstrosities in the course of their lives, who promptly had to be battled.

At the latest by the age of five I had to have been well versed in all the black-white stereotypes, to the point where I had acquired so many complexes that I asked my foster mother to wash me white, and secretly ate soap. My white playmates, however, felt very comfortable in their skin. Is it any wonder? They experienced life as little, soon to be grown-up, conquerors, pioneers, explorers, and masters, seeing it as completely normal.

Even though that was thirty years ago, the same forms and substance of racist erasure and discrimination still exist. When I see Afro-German children living in the city of Berlin and particularly in Germany's rural areas, I wonder what kinds of games they might be playing at home, in pre-school and at school. What kinds of strategies will they develop at some point to assert themselves in a society that externally appears to be multicultural but internally is racist. A society in which anti-Semitism remains virulent and where colonialism is a chapter of national history too eagerly silenced. Who and where are the contemporary models of Afro-German children and youth? Who are their identity symbols, whom do they relate to? What do they learn about their heritage and what of the history of black people in Europe and on other continents? Where and how do they meet black people in their immediate environment? What black-white stereotypes are they taught from the public media and through play and educational materials? Do they manage, with all their other childhood fears and problems, to put up with the enormous burden of everyday racism?

Racist Speech as a Normative Stress Factor

Concerning the everyday experiences of a six-year-old black child his Ghanaian mother reports:

> *When he used to be called "nigger" in pre-school,*
> *he realized that this term contained something*
> *negative. This business of being called nigger*
> *haunted us all the time. Everywhere we would go*
> *children would start shouting: "Nigger. Nig-*
> *ger." And the way they said it and then quickly*
> *ran away, even a child would have to notice that*
> *there was something in this word that was wrong,*
> *that they wanted to annoy us. One day something*
> *strange happened: Kofi asked me, "Mama, do*
> *you want to marry a white man someday?" I was*
> *totally surprised and asked, "Why?, What do you*
> *mean?" And he said, "Well, you know, Mama,*
> *then he'll call us niggers." That was really sad, I*
> *thought.*[5]

Racist speech is something that black people of any age have to deal with daily. The word "nigger" is only one such example. Constantly, black people are expected to accept and patiently put up with casual use of terms which, in light of social developments and progressive debate, are now considered offensive language. Since the "Black Power Movement" of the 1960s whites ought to be aware that people of African descent have been objecting to the term "nigger," since this expression is a symbol of contempt and enslavement of blacks. It is precisely the colloquial use of the word "nigger" that illuminates its covert content: "I'm not your nigger, you know" (flunky, servant, slave). For children any newly introduced term is neutral at first; but in the course of their socialization they learn very soon what can be expressed with that choice of language. Before they consciously understand it, they sense the hidden innuendoes concealed behind the terms:

> *For example, when I would play with kids in pre-*
> *school, then I was the nice lady, but the moment I*
> *commanded them to do something they didn't*
> *want to do, then I was suddenly a nigger. They'd*
> *shout: "Nana nana boo boo, you are a nigger."*[6]

A further source of stress is the fact that, in contending with language, it usually isn't enough that black people repudiate and reject certain expressions as racist; they are expected to explain why, with patience and diplomacy. And sometimes, on top of that, they even have to put up with the accusation of being too "sensitive," as in "But you know I didn't mean it that way"; or "I know one black person who doesn't mind that term and even uses it himself." Attempts to soften racism, coupled with ignorance and lack of respect is sometimes more injurious than the racist content of a word or phrase.

The "Berlin Institute for Advanced Training and School Development" included in its 1994 manual "Little Games" the song "Ten Little Niggers," not by accident, but consciously as a recommended singing and movement game, accompanied by instructive notes: "Pupils can be given the aural task of noting how the niggers are eliminated," a recommendation which is obviously out of the question. "Written in the colonial mentality of the 19th century," states the book *Showing Our Colors* ironically, "the widely disseminated and popular song of the 'Ten Little Niggers" is one of many that presents the deficiencies and inferiority of Africans in a form suited to children. As doubly trivialized beings, the *'little* niggers,' are transposed into German or European circumstances, and in every situation where their ability to adapt is put to the test, they fail."[7]

Thus through lively melody and catchy rhythm ethnocentric ideas of superiority are inculcated into white children, and in black children, a consciousness of their inferiority.

Stress of Conforming in Upbringing, School, and Work

For brown-skinned people significant stress is caused by the need to explain themselves at every turn, to be constantly on guard against verbal or physical attacks, and never to be able to express themselves or move spontaneously. Bikai D., of Cameroon, explains:

> *I think that as an African or black there is never a moment that you're not being observed. Whenever I go out for a walk or shopping I notice that people I encounter are observing exactly what I'm wearing, whether I behave in any special way, and that they look me straight in the eye. When I stare back at them, they look away.*[8]

Fashion trends proclaim attention-getting extravagance. However, what for white Germans is a choice that brings occasional or even frequent pleasure is for blacks often an involuntary and on-going stress: The Afro-German woman J.D. says, on this point:

> *It used to really bother me that I stood out everywhere. Even now it still does sometimes but not to the same degree: For example, I'm careful not to dress in bright, noticeable colors. Most of the clothes I have are in grays and blues.*[9]

As early as pre-school training and socialization Afro–German children are generally expected to be able to conform, to be subordinate, patient, and understanding. Especially in those areas where only few black people live, they are constantly reminded by their caregivers to be careful not to draw attention to themselves in any way. Helga Emde grew up in the post-War period:

I had to be careful not to be conspicuous or else I'd be noticed, not as a sassy little girl but as 'nigger,' 'moorhead,' 'Sarotti-Moor.' I wasn't to be conspicuous under any circumstances, but I had always been 'big and husky' for my age. I was not supposed to be conspicuous, and yet I was noticeable to everybody with my frizzy hair and my black skin.[10]

Given the stereotype that blacks are supposed to be intellectually less stimulated and capable, well-meaning and ambitious teachers are often motivated to have Afro-Germans prove the opposite. They are expected to be above average in effort, neatness, propriety, intelligence, cleanliness and behavior.

My mother and grandmother grew up in Germany as Afro-Germans. In order to escape prejudices against Africans, they brought me up to be especially clean and neat and to perform especially well at school and in my occupation. I had to be better than the others or at least at the top of the heap.[11]

Nevertheless, exceptional achievement is often viewed with skepticism by the white world:

I had been trained as a foreign-language secretary and was now making applications in writing and by phone. They ask for statistics: age, nationality. In my head wheels started turning. Can I show up there with my Berlin accent and my skin color? Did the inquiry about nationality arise because of my last name, Adomako? I go to one of the many interviews. Brilliant machinations take place to hide xenophobia and preju-

dice....When I'm finally hired, it continues; I
sense the prejudice of colleagues and superiors.
"You wrote that wrong." Doubts about my abili-
ty. Africans just can't do this. But I trained in
this occupation. Then I don't know who's right
anymore.[12]

This Afro-German woman's commentary demonstrates that
stress arises not only when others doubt one's capabilities; it
arises also because these usually unjustified doubts must constantly be tested and because there are usually no other blacks
available to affirm or vindicate one's own self-actualization.

Something that Afro-German women and men experienced early in their childhood was a kind of direct or indirect
guidance to prepare themselves for a life outside Germany,
there being virtually no occupational future for them here. Or
they have to settle for employment on the German job market
unsuited to their training and qualifications, but conforming to
the society's expectations: Blacks are musicians, athletes, and
employed in the service occupations. Their accomplishments
are readily lauded as "natural talent," but less readily as individual accomplishment when they really are, in accordance with
those expectations, engaged in the entertainment or sports professions and do succeed. Janine D. tells her experience:

Many people believe that I must have a very good
singing voice, which isn't so. In a disco, when
there's a reggae piece, people will expect me to
jump onto the dance floor. If I don't, then they
usually make a remark about it being "my"
music.[13]

I'm always amazed at how many black Germans are employed
in caregiving establishments, women primarily in elderly and

nursing care.

The limited occupational and professional spectrum is not accidental and often only appears to be a matter of free choice. Given the disadvantaged status of women in the larger society and the complex web of racism and sexism, discrimination and exclusion have a special impact on black women. Careers, influential positions and civil service posts are categorically denied them. Black women have to fight simultaneously against racism and sexism, which aggravates their situation in comparison to that of black men.

Insitutionalized and individual discrimination can be found in women-centered situations as well: In feminist projects and counseling services immigrant women are frequently interpreters, regardless of their expertise; sometimes under the pretext of deficient skills or lack of certification they are relegated to all those job categories and menial jobs that no woman would like to have. Seldom do they have permanent, well-paid positions; far more often they work with short-term contracts or in federally created job-corps situations. Most often white women hold a monopoly over the distribution of jobs and, as project initiators and/or directors, claim certain privileges without inquiring whether an immigrant or black German woman ever had or could have the chance to arrive at such a position as they.

The setting of quotas, needed to rectify the general disadvantages to women, extend to immigrant and black German women only in exceptional cases. Compared with immigrant women, especially those of darker skin, black German women might seem "privileged"; however, for sure, compared with white Germans, they are employed to a disproportionately high percentage in types of jobs that entail greater physical exertion and toxic exposure as well as greater risk of accidents. Apart from those factors there are also subtle and overt disadvantages, racist behaviors and attitudes that affect the professional and everyday life of black people who are situated in highly visible professions and positions. According to W.A., an African psychiatrist:

> *Daily I get the question: 'How can a black person from Africa do therapy?"…There are psychoanalysts who consider me incapable of treating German patients, meaning, from a psychoanalytic perspective. As a primary argument, they bring up culture and language. Apparently, I cannot understand the cultural identity of my patients; I have a different mentality from whites, i.e., moody, aggressive, instinctual, impressionable. What this is saying is that, those analysts are arguing from ideas that were accepted as valid a hundred yeas ago, such as those of Malinowski, when knowledge was shaped by colonialism: 'The "Negro" is incapable of thought.'*[14]

White Stress—East/West

Afro-Germans who grew up in the GDR have experiences similar to those of black Germans in the FRG when it comes to day-to-day racism. Even though, by virtue of state sanctions against racism, they were very seldom confronted with open discrimination, the official programs of "international solidarity" were, however, decreed from above. Nor was there any fundamental assessment of the German colonial past. Since private contacts between foreigners and GDR citizens were prevented to the best of the state's ability to do so, black people suffered far greater isolation and aloneness. Black Germans were, as such, perceived as "foreigners":

...in the GDR I was taken to be from Africa or Cuba. In the GDR it was clear that I wasn't of North American origin, anyway; that's rare there.

...it was made blatantly clear to me that I was a foreigner and that I am not viewed as a German. In the smaller towns it's very strong, but in East Berlin, too, people would turn around and look at me: "Hey, look." I have no feeling of "home," because this pressure from outside was so great.[15]

Due to restrictions on travel, Afro-Germans in the GDR could rarely stay in touch with their black parent, if he had left the country, and/or establish connections with other black relatives. When the Wall between the two German states came down, black Germans, even as GDR citizens, still remained largely invisible, unheard, and unasked, when it came to experiences before, during, and after the so-called re-unification. In both parts of the now-unified Germany the "oversexed" stereotype not only denies black women and men intellectual ability, it also slanders black men as rapists and black women as loose sex objects. This means that black people have to deal not only with exclusion in all areas of public life; in personal friendships and intimate relationships, too, racist stereotypes can become a stress factor:

I've come to the conclusion that there is an image held by many men that a woman of color is easier to "bed down." So I'm much more likely to be approached, and more directly, than white women friends. It happens over and over; consequently I'm doubly suspicious when someone is interested in me.[16]

Black people are conspicuous in the street scene of the old and new German states, but at the same time they experience being "overlooked" everywhere, being quasi non-existent. No matter whether it has to do with skin cosmetics or hair brushes, band-aids, or any sort of prosthesis—the big and small things of life are exclusively fitted to the needs of white people: "Flesh-colored" means "white'; hair is basically more or less straight. On this subject, the experience of the Afro-American writer Audre Lorde after her mastectomy in a New York hospital:

> *The next day a kindly woman from Reach for Recovery came in to see me, with a very upbeat message and a little prepared packet containing a soft sleep-bra and a wad of lambswool pressed into a pink breast-shaped pad....I looked away, thinking, 'I wonder if there are any black lesbian feminists in Reach for Recovery?'*[17]

Stress through Isolation

Compared to countries with a large black population the situation of people of African descent in Germany is exacerbated by the fact that they must deal with prejudices and discrimination all by themselves, without back-up from a strong "community" that functions as a lobby. In dealing with daily life and work, they are often entirely on their own and, hence, are treated as representatives of an imagined group: surprise in finding differences in skin color and socialization among Afro-Germans and/or that they don't know each other; "I know another Afro-German, but she's not at all like you"; "I once had a friend from Ghana; his name is Kofi and he lives in Berlin. Do you know him?"

My own self-awareness as an Afro-German woman underwent a positive change in the mid-80s by getting to know and networking with other Afro-Germans. Isolation had produced in me the effect of experiencing myself as a foreign body within the West German society. Within my foster family and during my school and university years, with my dark skin and German socialization, I was in a position where I rarely found people to talk to who I felt could really understand me. Afro-Germans are always supposed to be accommodating with explanations about ancestry, identity, and skin color. What's more, if they respond with anger and annoyance, then they're usually accused of being oversensitive or even arrogant.

For years I lived with the sense of having neither a history nor a future in German society, but rather of eventually having to emigrate. That this is burdensome is obvious. In the meantime, I realize that this is not a singular experience, but that mine is a prime example of the interaction with a sector of the population, which, in the consciousness of parts of the German society, simply does not exist— an experience that is also relevant for those Afro-Germans who grew up in the former GDR and/or live in the new federal states.

A visible and strong "community" creates protection against isolation, if not against discrimination as well. It can also provide anonymity and individuality, as well as the possibility to choose, from among other black people, friends, role models, and people to whom one can relate. What I have the greatest need for in all parts of Germany is the group of older black people. The few African and Afro-German senior citizens live widely dispersed and often alone among white retirees of their age. What is their day-to-day life in German rest homes like?

Racism as Stress Factor in Psychosocial Emergencies

What is it like for black people, even younger ones, who live in psychiatric institutions? For people of African descent and black Germans who find themselves in acute crisis situations, there is no place free of racism. Psychiatrist and psychoanalyst W.A. kindly gave me access to his notes on case studies:

> *Dr. A, from East Africa, was admitted to the psychiatric clinic after having exhibited behavioral disorders....There were major problems concerning responsibility for payment for the in-patient treatment of the psychically abnormal doctor. Among the comments were the following: "We can't be responsible for all blacks. If we assume all the costs for him, then the whole African continent will be coming to us. The niggers ought to stay where they came from ...." On the ward tensions developed between this patient and others. Because the patient, in his disorientation, took to gathering up everything, food included, staff members asserted: "In the Sahel region there's no food, so he has to collect for all the niggers." During the night the patient was beaten up by fellow patients, sustaining injuries in the genital area, among others. He was removed to the surgical ward, where he died during surgery. He was 34 years old.*[18]

Psychiatrist W.A. expressed fear, as an African, of racist persecution in the event of publication of the cited commentary. A fear that is by no means imaginary, it unquestionably lends to the topic under discussion a further dimension of social and political volatility. There are very few mental health institutions in Germany where the health and counseling services devote themselves to issues and problems related to migration and racism. Even when demand and opportunities for therapy have skyrocketed such that there is talk of a "psychoboom," there is still no consideration whatsoever of opportunities where immigrants or black Germans can find therapeutic support. While white Germans are confronted with the dilemma of having to choose from an enormous field of therapy possibilities, black Germans and immigrants have trouble finding information about therapy opportunities, not to mention having choices. Psychologists and therapists feel they are not responsible, not prepared, and not competent to meet these "special" needs. Scrutinizing literature on the subject of immigration and health I notice that culturally determined differences in connection with psychic and psychosomatic complaints of immigrants are sometimes accorded an openly negative, but often subtly condescending value. This applies especially to people of non-European descent. Hence, Laffrachini appears neither to interpret his patients' neuroses in their social context nor to take them seriously at all:

> *In just this state of anxiety and insecurity all manner of pathological ideas emerge and take shape in their* primitive *and* magical *imagination. Those ideas are in direct relationship to their upbringing and educational level. ... To regain their manhood the patients are prepared to give up everything: "Professor, if you cure me, I'll give you all my savings, I'll give you anything you want!"*[19]

Most available cases examining the mental-health situation of immigrants and black Germans are based on medical and symptomatic interpretations. Very seldom do social scientists candidly state their research interests and self-critically reflect upon their own position and assessment methodologies. Nevertheless, if, often, we find reference to differences in the manifestation and handling of illnesses, there remains a lack of guidance and examples explaining how such differences can be appropriately incorporated, and where the possibilities and limits of therapeutic efficacy lie. Frequency and characteristics of individual illnesses are the focus of interest, but not the personal and social circumstances within which these illnesses develop. The result is, then, that, instead of pursuing the causal factors for the illness, it is often the patients themselves that become problematized. Psychiatrist W.A. writes:

> *At present I have a forty-three-year-old Afro-German patient, who, as a child, was abandoned by his mother in a tote bag.... This patient was previously seen by a white German neurologist, who was, in my opinion, not competent even for white Germans. He asserted that "'mix-raced people are bound to have problems anyway, and that those problems are not treatable by therapy, because they are race-mentality-specific'" With this explanation he sent the patient away.*[20]

Black Stress in the Everyday White Environment

In addition to all these stress factors there is also the fact that we as blacks place tremendous pressure upon each other: We expect each other to avoid all the faults that we criticize in whites; we would like to see other blacks cool-headedly deal with racism and discrimination, that they serve as role-models and allies for us, and that those who hold influential positions not only perform well in their professional sphere but beyond that, represent as spokespersons and activists the interests of the black population. A black person appearing in front of the camera, for example, is expected not to "disgrace" other blacks through over-assimilation, arrogance, or deficient qualifications. This means that, sometimes, we unconsciously take on the society's racism and its strictures. Often we are much stricter, much more merciless, and more demanding in our dealings with other blacks than with whites. Furthermore, we often have difficulty tolerating our diversity of ancestry, skin color, socialization or political consciousness. We wish to see ourselves as one, but we aren't. Some of us have managed, for example, to live in a racist environment by assimilating quite well, while others in similar circumstances have become rebellious. Many Afro-Germans have a great deal of access to other people of African descent, while others lack even the slightest contact with their black family members. Black Germans cannot wrap themselves in either the African nor the German part of their heritage, and so are forced to develop a self-awareness that draws its strength neither from insider nor from outsider status. This is something that actually needs to be learned as well by whites who have previously been able to take privilege and power for granted.

White Stress and Black Nerves: What to Do About It?

Our lives as black people in a society that perceives itself as "white" will be more stress-free if we can reach out more to each other, accept each other and learn from each other. The more we know about our history and present, the less others can "whitewash" us. At the same time the feeling of isolation will subside if we form contacts with other blacks within and outside of Germany, particularly those of the older generation.

It is important that we as black people create spaces in which we can be among "ourselves," in order to comprehend our commonalties and differences, to exploit them in our everyday lives and political work. But also, just for once not to be confronted with white racism, to create some moments of relaxation and release for ourselves. For the dismantling of institutionalized discrimination we must constantly, but selectively, enter into coalitions with as many marginalized groups as possible and with progressive whites to push, for example, for anti-discrimination legislation and job quotas. Collective action is not only more effective, it also conserves strength and can even be enjoyable.

Notes

1. Chris Lange, "Evatöchter wider Willen. Feministinnen und Religion," in: Ika Hügel et al (eds.), *Entfernte Verbindungen. Rassismus, Antisemitismus, Klassenunterdrückung.* Berlin 1993, p. 99.
2. May Opitz (Ayim), "Afro-Deutsche. Ihre Kultur- und Sozialisationsgeschichte auf dem Hintergrund gesellschaftlicher Veränderungen." Master's thesis, University of Regensburg 1986, p. 121.
3. May Opitz (Ayim), Katharina Oguntoye, Dagmar Schultz, eds., *Showing Our Colors: Afro-German Women Speak Out* (Anne V. Adams, transl.) Amherst, UmassP, 1991, p. 61.
4. May Opitz (Ayim), "Ethnozentrismus und Geschlecterrollenstereotype in der Logopädie." Lehranstalt für Logopädie, Berlin, 1984.
5. Gisela Fremgen (ed.),...*und wenn du dazu noch schwarz bist. Berichte schwarzer Frauen in der Bundesrepublik*, Bremen, 1984.
6. Fremgen, p. 37
7. Opitz et al, p.127-8
8. Opitz, "Afro-Deutsche," p. 117.
9. Opitz, , "Afro-Deutsche," p. 131.
10. Opitz et al., p. 102.
11. Opitz et al., p. 199.

12. Opitz et al., p. 201-2.

13. Opitz, "Afro-Deutsche," p. 131.

14. W.A. "Falldarstellungen zum Rassismus in der psychiatrischen Praxis." North-Rhein Westfalia 1990 (unpublished ms.)

15. Opitz et al. p., 153, 154.

16. Opitz, "Afro-Deutsche," p. 132.

17. Audre Lorde, *Cancer Diaries.* (San Francisco: Spinsters Ink: 42)

18. W.A., "Falldarstellungen."

19. Vera Götz, *Physische und psychische Erkrankungen bei Arbeitsmigranten in der BRD.* Gelsenkirchen 1986, p. 158.

20. W.A., "Falldarstellungen."

insignificant

22nd september 19 hundred and sometime
a completely ordinary day
in a lower district court somewhere

the man behind the desk
greets politely and
discreetly reports
as is appropriate for a civil servant
sitting in a public office

he doesn't need a name
— just as I thought —
but only my number
4 VI 2 9 3 8
from the guardianship papers

he opens a book
he shakes his head
he closes the book
he says suddenly:

      destroyed

the file on your life
that began in 1960
as soon as you
came of age

      was burned

the door in front of me opens
"thanks" i say softly
and closes behind me again

the file knew more about me than
i know about the past

22nd september 19 hundred and sometime
here and there
ashes drop from the sky
black tears fall
into a completely ordinary day

1992

(Translation by Ekpenyong Ani; from *blues in schwarz weiss*)

the nervous costume

it is pretty and ugly
and from the sixties
used to be drip an' dry then
and durable
wrinkle-free and behaved
inconspicuously

it was given to me
at birth

unfortunately it was only
short and seldom
mine alone
quite soon everyone
pounced upon it
and made fun of it

for years
especially parents and teachers
tugged at it
with good intentions
and impatience
they cut off
the ragged edges

when they
finally let go
others I did not know
hung on my apron strings

some were nice
and became friends
but the closest ones
became the worst
nuisances

some friends
soon became
strangers again
and others even sooner
cheated on me

in the seventies
life was quite fun
meanwhile I had become
completely frayed
but that was in style at the time
and cool in summer

in the early eighties
all the fringes fell off
and the whole rag
has become
full of holes and most of all
hairy
I even talked
my head off
till no-one could
listen anymore

since then
not much has changed
except that by now
I am left

almost naked
one of the nuisances
has recently
ruined
my costume completely

if you
could spare
a bunch of nerves
I would be grateful
in case you
have been robbed
of your last nerve
as so many have
I share
my nervousness

5-3-1995

(Translation by Ekpenyong Ani; from *nachtgesang*)

Racism and Oppression in Unified Germany

In 1991 the "Fifth Intercultural Summer Institute for Black Women's Studies" took place in Berlin, Bielefeld, and Frankfurt/Main. It was the first time that an international conference on this topic was held in Germany, an important milestone especially for the black women living here. The 1994 publication Schwarze Frauen der Welt *[Black Women of the World] includes the following contribution by May Ayim.*

The topic "Racism and Oppression in Unified Germany" is not only very broadly conceived but also grounded in two distinct perspectives: Until recently the FRG and the GDR were two geographically and ideologically separate nations, a fact demonstrated, yesterday as well today, in current manifestations of and responses to racism.

I myself have lived only in West German cities and on the west side of Berlin; this sets the focus and emphasis of my remarks.

I grew up in the 1960s in suburban and small-town North-Rhine Westphalia, in a white German foster family. I had four white siblings and was the second-oldest of the five of us. The 1960s were a period when many men and women mainly from neighboring European countries were recruited for employment in the FRG. In 1955 the FRG's first contract for this purpose was signed with Italy, followed, in the 1960s, by contracts with Spain, Greece, Turkey, Portugal, Tunisia, Morocco, and Yugoslavia.

This recruitment began at a time when there were 1.2 million unemployed in the FRG. Apparently these jobless people could not be placed, and obviously, it was more profitable for industry to recruit foreigners than to configure the job market more attractively for the domestic pool. In this way industrials could maintain—or even introduce—poor working conditions (e.g. shift-work, piecework, assembly-line work, and night work). The federal government and German entrepreneurs regarded the immigrants not primarily as people but as an expendable work force which, hopefully, depending on economic conditions, would leave or come back to the country. "Rotation principle" was the official slogan for the shuttle movement being fostered, and "guest worker" was the polite euphemism for the fact that, for the "invitees" no permanent stay was planned.

Not until the beginning of the 1970s were any efforts made toward so-called integration measures. This included, for example, supplemental teacher training for working with immigrant children. Government programs were rarely intended to be accommodating by assuming from the outset the task of easing immigrants' adjustment. More often measures were after-the-fact reactions to actual realities and to hostility that was gradually coming out into the open. Above all, in the course of the economic crises in the late 1960s and early 1970s, latent racism came to the surface and manifested itself in expressions like "Out, foreigners!" and in the expansion of radical-right ideologies.

Integration measures were aimed at avoiding social conflicts and required the one-way adaptation of the immigrants to German conditions despite continued denial of civil rights (e.g. voting rights). Thinking back on my childhood, even though I don't recall immigrant workers in my specific environment, I do remember often hearing expressions like "Spaghetti-eaters" used as a derogatory term for Italians, or the claim that nearly all foreigners work in the garbage business.

It is still a fact that the majority of jobs with the lowest pay and the most dangerous working conditions are held by immigrants. Even though the workers recruited at that time were carefully selected according to occupational and health criteria, those criteria bore no relevance to the deplorable jobs that awaited them. The selection processes in themselves were degrading and sexist anyway. The category "viably healthy" was one criterion, for example, that meant a woman must not be pregnant. If a woman who had entered were found to be pregnant, then she could be sent back to her country of origin at the state's expense. The German employer had virtual re-call rights. Further grounds for exclusion included advanced tooth decay, periodontal disease, hearing and vision impairment.

Even though it may have seemed so for many, in actuality most of the people from foreign countries residing in the FRG were not really in a position to determine "freely" whether and when they would come. They are not tourists. They left their country fleeing hunger, war, persecution and expulsion and/or in search of work and educational opportunities. Just because in Europe, due to the Gulf War—for a short time!— war, fear, and threat suddenly became current topics of conversation, this does not mean that most people on this globe had been living in peace for the previous decades.

My father came to Germany from Ghana at the end of the 1950s to attend the university. In 1957, Ghana became the first African country to achieve the democratic status of independence. In the years that followed increasing numbers of Africans came to Germany from other African countries, mainly students at first; since then, mainly refugees.

My father came and did not stay.

I always knew him better from hearsay than from actual acquaintance; for a long time I was the only black person in my environment. My first encounters—along with my foster-family siblings—with other black people came through the imaginary world of children's books and songs: "Uncle Tom's Cabin" and the "Ten Little Niggers," for example.

The conception that I got as a child from the grown-ups' world was: Black people are funny-looking; they are sort of ugly, frightening, and not too smart. Or they grin a lot, are very nice and friendly but still not too smart.

Somewhere along the way I must also have seen myself. It was easier for me to identify with white princesses than with characters who looked like me. I hadn't even started school when I asked my foster mother to wash me white. I had already learned the first lesson in racism: white is better!

When my African father one day stood at our door in real life, it was the sensation and terror of the whole neighborhood, and the scare of the day for my friends and playmates. Some ogled open-mouthed and whispered, hands covering their mouths; others ran away in fear.

At school we learned—and by "we" I mean basically all of us who grew up in the FRG—nothing about the lives of immigrants in the FRG and nothing at all about black people in this country.

We didn't learn when and why the façade of friendliness toward immigrants turned into open hostility.

We didn't learn that the life sagas of Africans in Germany could be documented back to the Middle Ages and farther.

We didn't learn that the first African student earned his doctoral degree with a dissertation about blacks in Europe—and not in the year 1967 but in 1729!

And we didn't learn that, during Nazi times, black Germans were persecuted, forcibly sterilized, expelled, and murdered.

We heard about Carl Peters, called "Hangman Peters," because in the German East African colonies he killed the most blacks per day.

We heard about "natives," "cannibals," and the gruesome "wild men," who were "developed" from "barbarism" to "civilization" by the "great deeds of European explorers."

Even today, they should still be developing. Depending on the masters' agenda and skill at packaging, oppression is glossed over and impoverishment dressed up as "authenticity."

In other words: on the subjects of colonial history, National Socialism, and racism, at school we were totally misinformed and rendered ignorant.

Many migrant workers of the first wave have since reached retirement age. The first Turkish seniors' club was opened in 1987 in Bielefeld.

At the moment more than five million immigrants live in the now reunified Germany. Over 80 percent of the so-called foreigners have lived here for more than ten years, and 60 percent of their children were born here. Yet Germany still does not perceive itself as a country of immigration; black and German are still considered as an exotic combination. Anyone who doesn't look typically German—which means essentially the Aryan ideal—apparently doesn't belong here.

Several years ago, when I met an Afro-German woman who was born in Hamburg in 1895, I myself was amazed. Since then, I take it for granted that many black Germans have long had grandchildren and great-grandchildren.

This also indicates that a lot has changed for me, too, in the past few years. Mainly from work on the book *Farbe Bekennen*, that Dagmar Schultz, Katharina Oguntoye, and I edited, my consciousness of myself and as a black person in Germany has changed considerably. Since then there have arisen organized groups of black Germans in a number of cities, in the East as well as the West of Germany; and even if the black community in this country is small, it is there, active, and constantly growing.

Unification of the GDR and the FRG has thus far not had much of a positive impact on immigrants, exiles, Jews, and black Germans, but rather has evidenced much more open and growing racism and anti-Semitism. At the moment, racist violence, especially in the five new federal states, is an everyday fact of life; and at the initial East-West celebrations our participation wasn't asked anyway. North-South was suddenly out.

Only for the election campaign did "multicultural" appear on the program. But the fact that we are "out" does not mean that we are no longer around. And just because we only get invited for "our" topics—racism, immigration law, residence issues, etc—does not mean that we won't insinuate ourselves everywhere and anyhow.

"Racism and Oppression" is going to be a current topic in Germany for the foreseeable future, which is both significant and frightening. However, I don't take it as a reason for resignation but rather a challenge to stronger action, including, for example, creating more and better strategies and coalitions, national as well as international. And for this, as Audre Lorde says, we don't have to be friends but have to learn to work together.

Since 1992 the borders between European countries have been falling. Simultaneously preparations are moving ahead in all European countries to shut themselves off even more than before from the countries of the so-called "Third World," which are still being held in a state of dependency.

Restrictive laws are increasingly limiting immigration, residence rights and employment possibilities for exiles and immigrants in all European countries. In addition, everyday racism threatens the lives of those who must fear being expelled or deported.

We are not "minorities," the ones they'd like to discriminate against. No, we are the majorities.

References

Lorde, Audre: *A Burst of Light: Essays by Audre Lorde*. Ithaca, Firebrand, 1988.

May Opitz (Ayim), Katharina Oguntoye, Dagmar Schultz, eds., *Showing Our Colors: Afro-German Women Speak Out* (Trans. Anne V. Adams.) Amherst, UMassP, 1991.

liberty of the arts

comments
of two authors
modified slightly in the wording
but true to the original content

Ms K.:

>   you may
>   take the word
>   "negro" or "mulatto"
>   as offensive
>   i cannot share your opinion for
>   i did not mean it offensively
>
>   for me such words sound
>   melodic and classical
>   tangibly sensual instead of inaccessibly objective
>
>   my creativity remains untouched by criticism of me
>   i have never once felt shame for anything
>
>   one of my pieces is titled
>   "foreigners welcome"
>   so i can't be
>   racist...

Ms S.:

>   i am disappointed in how few west german publishers
>   show interest in east german authors

they only publish their own stuff
or books by foreigners or mulattos
that's not just neglect
it's also cheating
apparently we're
not exotic enough...

1992

(Translation by Ekpenyong Ani; from *blues in schwarz weiss*)

autumn in germany

it is not true
that it is not true
that's how it was
first at first and then again

that's how it is

"kristallnacht":
in november 1938
first shattered
were windowpanes
then
again and again
human bones
of jews and blacks
of the weak and the sick
of sinti and roma and
poles of lesbians and
gays of and of
and of and of
and and

first a few then many

more and more:
arms lifted and joined in
applauded clapping
or stealthily gaping
as they
and them
and he and she

and him and her
first once in a while
then again and again

again so soon?

a singular incident:
in november 1990
antonio amadeu from angola
was murdered
in eberswalde
by neo-nazis
his child born shortly after by a
white german
woman
her house
shortly after
trashed

ah yes

and the police
came so late
it was too late
and the newspapers were so short
of words
it equaled silence
and on TV no picture
of this homicide

no comment on the incident:

in the newly united germany
that so much likes to

likes too much
to call itself re-united
it happened
that here and there
it was first houses
then people
that burnt down
first in the east then in the west
then
the whole country

first at first and then again

it is not true
that it is not true
that's how it was

that's how it is:
autumn in germany
i dread the winter

1992

(Translation by May Ayim/Ekpenyong Ani; from *blues in schwarz weiss*)

the accommodation

the ones with a say
say it's a home
it isn't
even a house

just a few walls
lots of people between them
a roof on top

no flowers
adorning the windows
now pictures on the wall
no carpet
neon light
day in day out

gray inside
the outside also
gray

fatima
searches for hands in the night
of her children
cries
startle her
from every dream

abroad
is loneliness
far away
is the homeland
no home

in germany united fatherland
another "refugee home"
was burnt down

roof and walls are gone
the people are dead
only ashes and smoke
charred
bones and skin

the ones with a say
say nothing
most of all others
remain silent
too

1993

(Translation by Ekpenyong Ani; from *nachtgesang*)

The Afro-German Minority

The dictionary Ethnische Minderheiten in der Bundesrepublik Deutschland [Ethnic Minorities in the Federal Republic of Germany] *was published in 1995. May Ayim wrote an entry on the historical and contemporary situation of Afro-Germans.*

Black Germans are usually viewed as "foreigners" even in the Federal Republic of the 1990s. Their residence in Germany is perceived as temporary; their social roots are connected often and exclusively to the Occupation period after World War II. "Afro-German" is a self-definition formulated in the early 1980s by German women of African and Afro-American descent, as an approach to questions of their identity, and has since come into wide usage.

With the term "Afro-German" it cannot and should not be a matter of exclusion on the basis of skin color; we know all too well what it means to suffer exclusion. More important, we want to propose "Afro-German" in opposition to more commonly used names like "half-caste," "mulatto," or "colored," as an attempt to define ourselves instead of being defined by others (Oguntoye et al, 1991, pp. xii-xiii).

The history of black people in Germany encompasses many generations. Over the centuries Blacks were continually coming to Germany; Caesar, for example, had Africans among his troops. In recent history, the Afro-German population can be broken down into several groups. The historical beginnings of the first generation are linked to Germany's colonial past. Since the census is rarely broken down according to skin color (a not unregrettable fact) it is impossible to ascertain how many Afro-Germans currently live in the FRG or how the numbers of this population have varied over the course of the centuries. It is worth noting that the degree of tolerance or

114

marginalization experienced by one sector of the population cannot be determined by its status as majority or minority in the society. South Africa, where a small 20-percent minority of whites has dominated the lives of an 80-percent black majority, clearly shows that racism is not so much a question of "minority" and "majority" as a question of privilege and power.

The History of Blacks in Germany and of Black Germans

During the Crusades, in the struggle against Islam, the Ethiopians, Christianized since the 4th century, were considered hopeful allies. Christian Blacks were therefore a frequent motif of saintly legends in medieval art and literature. Since the 12th century, when the skeletons of the Three Magi were transferred from Italy to Germany, one of the kings has been represented in the figure of Caspar as a black man. Positive representations of black people begin to decrease, however, with the incursion of Islam into the African continent and in the course of colonial projects. The term "moor," the defining label for black people in common usage up until the 18th century, reflects mostly religious-based prejudices and antipathy toward blacks as people of African origin and as "heathens."

Western-Christian color symbolism, since time immemorial, has associated the color black with the abominable and the undesirable. Accordingly, examples can be found in early literature where white people become "moors" for wrongful behavior. In the ecclasiastical vocabulary of the Middle Ages the terms "Aethiops" and "Aegyptius" were used to a remarkable degree as synonyms for the concept of the Devil. Religiously based prejudices and discrimination thereby formed a part of the foundation from which in colonial times a conglomeration of racist convictions could easily evolve, making black heathens (moors) into black subhumans (niggers).

Stereotyped ideas and mystifying representations of people of African descent can be traced back to medieval times. Then, German contacts with Africa were confined largely to financial participation in trade relations. In particular, the trading companies Fugger, Welser and Imhoff financed some of the first fleets that engaged in trade under Portuguese and Spanish flags. In this manner Africans, too, were brought to Germany as exotic souvenirs and placed in fashionable homes as servants.

At the dawn of the colonial era, in particular, the achievements and contributions of people of African descent were pushed into the shadows, suppressed and eradicated from white historiography. Even facts about the life course of Africans and Afro-Germans who managed to escape the normally prescribed servant's existence are accessible only in isolated sources and must be tediously culled. Few, however, attained high social status, e.g., the Afro-German Princess Charlotte Sophia, wife of the English king George III in the 18th century, or Anton Wilhelm Amo, from what is now Ghana, who in the early 18th century grew up in the house of the Duke of Wolfenbuettel, attended school and earned a doctorate at the University of Halle. Amo was named by Fredrick Wilhelm I to the Council of State of the Prussian crown and left Germany in 1743 because of increasing racist discrimination (see Brentjes 1977). Only in very recent times has it become known that the famous composer Ludwig van Beethoven (1770-1827) was of African heritage and had dark skin (Rogers 1952, p. 289).

Blacks in the Era of Enlightenment and Racial Ideologies

Rosemarie Lester, who has researched the image of blacks in the history of art, demonstrates that paintings from the 11th century until the time of colonial settlement gave generally accurate portraits of Africans and Afro-Germans. However, in the succeeding centuries up to the present, more and more graphic representations caricatured black people and/or presented them in an inaccurate social and historical context. The subjects of ethnologic observation and encounter became, in the Europe of the colonial era, objects of the Europeans' own imagination, interests and projections. Racist ideologies were developed in 17th and 18th century Europe, taking deep root during the Enlightenment, just at the time when revolutionary demands for freedom and equality ceased to be compatible with class privilege or a hierarchy of men over women. The promulgation of racist and sexist ideologies fulfilled the function of basing privileges that could no longer be defended as "divine will" on biological differences among people, hence re-codyifing them. Treatises on race theory were expressions of a constructed polarization based on social class, ethno-cultural background, and gender. Gustav Klemm, in his ten-volume publication on general cultural history, distinguished "active male" and "passive female" peoples. This theory holds that the former are peoples of discovery, invention and legal systems, while the latter are those who, from time immemorial, have lived their lives content and satisfied with their way of life and without political ambitions. On the basis of economic and political exploitation and superior weaponry technology, it was ultimately white male Europeans who set themselves as the measure of the master race. They were followed in rank by white women, then black men and black women in last position. Within Europe these racial theories legitimated social and gender privilege; outside Europe they justified the subjugation and annihilation of entire peoples and cultures as the "natural right" and "cultural mission" of the "higher race." With the demise of the estate society and the waning influence of the Church as normative authority, there were fewer and fewer religious values and aesthetic standards on which to base the denigration and marginalization of people of African descent and darker skin; in their stead were the approach and ethic that accompanied the rise of industrial capitalism. Other peoples and cultures were considered by ethnologists and anthropologists on the basis of their technical development in relation to the white European and classified as "barbaric," "primitive," and "uncivilized" — classifications still used today as supposedly neutral in referring to non-European cultures but which when applied to one's own person or population are perceived as insults.

With the rise of industrialization came the development of a mirror-image contrast to the barbarian-cannibal-subhuman theory in the popular stereotype of the "noble savage," characterized by gentleness and innocence, living a carefree and happy life. Like the projections driven by colonialist interests caricaturing Africans at best as children to be disciplined, those ideas bore little relationship to the actual reality of black people. They were much more the expression of a wistful longing in the ever more materially-oriented European world. Even with intentions of good will any ideas regarding African people were still based in condescending paternalism toward the "nature children," viewed both as immature and naïve. Rarely was any doubt evinced as to the Eurocentrically constructed hierarchy of human races, in which the highest position was ascribed to whites, even when strong criticism was occasionally applied to social relationships within Europe and colonial exploitation and slavery—criticism that by the 19th century was rarely voiced aloud, for the colonial mentality was drawing an ever-widening circle.

Blacks at the Height of German Colonialism

In 1884 at the Congress of Berlin the European powers divided up the African continent among themselves. Africa was not only to be taken over into European hands, but to be Europeanized and Christianized as well. Togo, Cameroon, German South-West Africa (Namibia), and German East Africa (Tanzania) became "internationally" recognized on this occasion by the other European powers as lawful German possessions. The boundaries drawn at this congress were determined purely by the military and economic interests of European statesmen and have retained their validity up to this day.

With increasing direct and indirect participation in the colonization of the African continent—particularly in the second third of the 19th century up to the forced relinquishing of the colonies at the end of the First World War—more and more Africans were "imported" to Germany. Exact figures are unavailable, "since the inhabitants of the former colonies or protectorates did not show up on the books as foreigners but as Germans ..." (Formal reply from the Federal Bureau of Statistics, 1987). While emigrant German men and women carried the consciousness of a national mission into the colonies, to educate the "natives" as "German subjects," black people in Germany had to submit to the pleasure of local society, often allowing themselves to be put on display through photographs or in person. As early as 1800 there were isolated cases of black people being stuffed and exhibited in natural history museums. In 1874, Carl Hagenbeck, during a lull in the animal business, exhibited human beings with such success that public exhibits of live persons subsequently became regular fare in waxworks, amusement parks and zoos(!). The German public feasted their eyes on the exotic presentations. Beyond that, scholars utilized members of different cultures for their studies and experiments, so that, next to monkeys and orangutans in their collections, "niggers," Hottentots, Chinese, Mongolians, and other preserved people were also employed to supplement "anthropological observations with their own live recollections" (Theye 1989, p. 103). Even young children were examined and abused in the interest of science. Concerning Theodor von Bischoff's studies of women in Tierra del Fuego, Ploss and Bartels reported, in 1913, (in Theye 1985, p. 263):

> *Only under resistance was he able to arrive at a very superficial perspective: even with the little three- and four-year-old girls of the troupe it was impossible for him to draw satisfactory conclusions as to the behavior of their sex organs, since their own resistance was supported by their mother. It was only when, a few weeks later, the Tierra del Fuegans, continuing their "Artistic Tour" through Europe, died in Switzerland from complications from colds, that von Bischoff was able to continue the examination on their corpses.*

Black Germans in the Weimar Republic

German colonial history was comparatively brief. However, in its content, intent and outcome it did not differ from other European colonial powers. The relinquishing of colonies was based not on humanitarian considerations and voluntary cession, but ensued as an imposed consequence connected with the defeat of the First World War. The colonial ethos, need for conquest, and belief in their master position remained undisturbed in Germany. Accordingly, wide circles of the German population and all political parties, with the exception of the USPD (Independent Socialist Party of Germany), protested against the presence of black soldiers in Germany, who were stationed, following the conclusion of the Treaty of Versailles, in the Rhineland along with French and Belgian occupation forces.

The retention and renewed mystification of the black person as "scapegoat" provided a welcome outlet to push white

Germans' violence into the shadows. In view of the putative dreadful brutality and sexual lust of blacks, any sexual offense by a white soldier or even of a civilian or husband appeared harmless by comparison.

Just as there was little general protest against the white occupation troops, the white children born of relationships between soldiers and German women drew equally little attention as problems. On the other hand, at the end of the 1920s considerations were discussed at government levels to send abroad children whose fathers were black soldiers and/or, by forced sterilization, prevent them from reproducing (cf. Pommerin 1979, p. 93f). The number of these black German children—often called "Rhineland bastards" as a matter of course during the Weimar Republic—was statistically recorded, from 1919, and, according to official figures, totaled 800 for the period up to 1945 (Eyferth et al. 1960, p. 11). The question of whether and how many black children who, in the absence of the protection of family or well-meaning welfare institutions, were already sterilized and/or sent away from the country during the Weimar Republic remains unknown.

Black Germans in the Era of National Socialism

According to estimates of the Swiss historian Micha Grin some 2,000 black people were interned in concentration camps by the National Socialists (*Jeune Afrique*, Oct. 9, 1990). Rainer Pommerin substantiates in his research that, between 1937 and 1942, at least 400 black Germans were forcibly sterilized. A small number of Afro-Germans survived the Holocaust because they were needed for propaganda purposes and therefore spared.

In order not to jeopardize diplomatic and commercial relations with foreign countries as well as colonial interests, the small group of African women and men from the former German colonies remained generally spared from State persecution. In contrast to them, most black Germans were not able to realize their educational aspirations and lost their jobs, if not also their lives.

Black Germans during the Occupation of the 1950s

Black German children born before and during the Rhineland occupation received no further special attention after the Second World War. The new statistics, papers, reports and studies concerned themselves exclusively with the next generation of black Germans. In 1952 the *International Federation for Services to Youth* (IFSY) in Geneva, in collaboration with German posts, conducted a census from which the number of children of occupation soldiers born between 1945 and 1951 was determined at 94,000, of whom 3,000 were black children (Frankenstein 1953, p. 95). In 1955 the Federal statistics gave the total number of "illegitimate children of colored extraction" as 4,776, which, however, included among the fathers not only "negroid"-looking U.S. military but also Puerto Ricans, Moroccans, Algerians, et. al. (Eyferth et al 1960, p. 11).

Even today black Germans are perceived in many places as "occupation babies," an ascription that is discriminatory on several accounts. Not only because the people so designated are forever regarded as "children" out of paternalistic condescension; behind the term "occupation baby" also lies the hidden, unsubstantiated, and generalized assumption that a black child, with a soldier of a foreign military force as a father, could not possibly be wanted. An "occupation baby"—at least a black one—is and remains, according to this view, a "problem."

In a questionnaire conducted in 1960 by Klaus Eyferth and other collaborators of the Psychological Institute of the

University of Hamburg it was shown that the society's prejudices against black Germans are nurtured by three sources:

> *Resentment toward the enemy occupation power,*
> *which, as a national prejudice, was automati-*
> *cally transmitted to black children, the visible*
> *offspring of the "invaders."*
>
> *Prejudice because of the social background of*
> *the children. Their mothers were blamed for the*
> *illegitimate birth and alleged that as "Ami-*
> *liebchen" [Yankee babes] they had taken up a sex-*
> *ual relationship with a black man only for the*
> *goods they could get. In early childhood this preju-*
> *dice was directed entirely at the mothers, while the*
> *children were seen to be cute and innocent. How-*
> *ever, in the expectation that "The apple doesn't*
> *fall far from the tree," later on the children*
> *would quickly be saddled with this prejudice.*
>
> *The prejudices, derived especially from*
> *inherited colonial, national socialist, and*
> *underlying racial ideologies, which hold that*
> *"mulattos" are genetically inferior and of lower*
> *intelligence.*

It is characteristic for the research and educational interests
of the 1950s that in discussing the social situation of black
Germans there was rarely any consideration of the white German population, which, by virtue of its racist past was still dis-
posed to marginalizing so-called "others." Even where
enlightened intent to ameliorate the situation of black children
did exist, the same biased paradigms that they set out to
improve upon show up clearly in the results of some studies. As
an example, for the procedure and evaluation of his study,
Kirchner uncritically relies on research on Africans in German

colonies and on anthropological studies carried out during the Nazi regime, commissioned to demonstrate the inferiority of people of African descent and to justify their cultural and physical annihilation. To illustrate, he referred to the study on "Crossing Europeans and Annamites" by Dr. W. Abel, who, as an expert, belonged to Special Commission 3, which, in 1937, directed the "discreet sterilization of the Rhineland bastards" as the measure was referred to. Furthermore, Kirchner interpreted his study results that proved developmental precociousness in Afro-German children in orphanages on the basis of suspect American research:

> *As for racial factors, we can infer that the developmental precociousness demonstrated by the mulatto children will probably stop at puberty. Particularly, intellectual capacity will most likely remain normal, according to available studies on American mixed-raced Negroes. On the other hand, one can infer that the strong sexuality observed in mulatto children will continue as a negroid racial indicator...(Kirchner 1952, p. 62).*

Black Germans in Media Coverage

In the spate of commentaries, as it were, on the situation of black Germans in media reportage from the 1950s to the early 1960s, emotions of pity and concern were evoked, as in the *Sonntagsblatt* of November 19, 1950, under the headline: "Children with a Heavy Lot." In 1952 the situation of black German children was discussed in Parliament to determine "whether it wouldn't be better for them to be sent to their fathers' countries..." (in: *Das Parlament*, Bonn 1952), since

124

the climatic conditions in Germany didn't suit them anyway.
Rosemarie Lester, analyzing the image of blacks in seven West
German illustrated magazines, concluded that the social situation of Afro-Germans here in the 1950s was processed for the
public as though it were a matter of not letting those "accidental products of a scandalous phenomenon suffer for the taint of
their dark skin" (Lester 1982, p. 110). Adolescent Afro-German girls born after the War were used increasingly after the
1960s by sex magazines for captions such as: "Drama of a
mulatto girl in Germany: She had to make love to all" (in *Pra-
line* 1972). Such captions capitalized primarily on the common stereotype of the putative sex drive of black women.

The Afro-German Situation since the 1960s

Over the course of the 1960s official interest in the collective
and individual situation of black Germans diminished, as
reflected in a sharp decline in publications. Simultaneously the
Afro-German population was growing, given that legal independence of African states enabled more and more Africans to
pursue studies at German universities.

It was a fact that in neither of the two Germanys was analysis of the colonial past on the agenda nor was the problemati-
zation of the racist and anti-Semitic past more than
superficially pursued. Hence, Afro-Germans in both Germanys continued to be confronted by unchanged stereotypes
about people of African descent and discriminated against in
their everyday lives.

The Situation of Black Germans in the Federal Republic

Since the economic crisis of the 1970s "dealing with foreigners" and "anti-foreigner sentiment" had become a consistently

recurrent theme in the Federal Republic. The specific situation of the black German population was hardly ever discussed, however, and then, primarily in connection with the growing number of African refugees in the Federal Republic. On this issue leading politicians had no reservations about spreading concepts like "flood of refugees" and "glut of foreigners" across the media landscape, thus effecting a radical rejection and exclusion of black people. Regarding the image of Africa in West German educational media Manfred Paeffgen writes:

> *Until about 1966 the African continent was considered mostly as an afterthought, even if a few attempts at a more basic revision of textbooks were undertaken....The disassociation from an ethnocentric evaluation of the non-European world was an element in a comprehensive critique of West German society....However, we cannot yet say that a change in the presentation of black Africa has been effected, though we can perhaps see movement toward a development (Paeffgen 1976, p. 240).*

With regard to their heritage, Afro-Germans find themselves confronted, even today, with the fact that they are seldom present in books for children and youth, nor are they in textbooks or literature for adults. Black people, insofar as they appear at all as protagonists in books and films, live mostly on other continents and are in large measure depicted as pitiful and needy and/or associated in image and language with attributes like "wild" and "uncivilized." Popular and leisure reading, in particular, depicted, since the 1950s and 1960s, an exceptionally hostile image of the independence movements in Africa. Above all, fear of the spread of communism was a recurrent theme, easily setting a background for representation of black freedom fighters as bloodthirsty terrorists.

Illustrations, texts, and songs that gained wide circulation in the spirit of the colonial mentality still enjoy, for the most part, uninterrupted popularity and are constantly being renewed. The song of the "Ten Little Niggers," for example, with its lively melody and children's language, conveys the idea that African men and women are not up to the requirements of so-called civilization. As beings not to be taken entirely seriously, also doubly diminutive "little bitty niggers," the children find one after the other dead. Like the Sarotti-Moor, popular trademark for several chocolate products, many consumer products that promote black people as exotic and as objects of desire are on the market. In this manner, from earliest childhood, racism becomes an everyday matter. Less intentionally evil than thoughtless, stereotypes that devalue black people and non-European lifestyles take root. Hence many a white German child, meeting an African or Afro-German for the first time, already has a pre-conceived image transmitted through children's books and songs. He or she has already tasted "Ice Cream Moors" and "Nigger Kisses," and learned to fear the "black bogeyman," the evil Knecht Ruprecht,* and has heard warnings about lies that turn the tongue and soul black, and played the game "Who's afraid of the black man?" Such messages and signals hinder a truly open encounter.

The high-tech media world makes it possible to follow news reports and events from all over the world. However, the interests of the powers-that-be and relevant filtering of information insures that knowledge is only selectively disseminated while myths and prejudices are stubbornly perpetuated. The German image of Africa and the view of black people still remains underdeveloped.

With regard to their life and history in the Federal Republic, Germans of African or Asian descent have been, up to the present, only seldom noticed, and up until the mid-1980s virtually not noticed at all. In the same way, "racism" was seldom spoken about. But black Germans were always included with refugees and immigrants when the talk was of the German people being saturated by foreigners.

Black Germans in the German Democratic Republic

Under the prescribed mantle of international solidarity, racist and anti-Semitic ideas blossomed in the GDR in a manner similar—if less obvious—to the situation in the FRG. The history and presence of black Germans was pushed into the background of forgetfulness here as well. Besides Africans who, as in the FRG, had been studying in the GDR in growing numbers since the 1960s, African men and women were coming from the beginning of the 1970s and completing training in skilled trades in the GDR on the basis of official state contracts. After the late 1970s and early 1980s it was primarily contract workers who immigrated into the GDR under the so-called governments' agreement. For these workers the term of residence was limited to a maximum of four to five years, coupled with the fact that their lodging in dormitories with strict visiting regulations was intended to, and did, hinder their contact with the local German population. "For GDR citizens there were no legal possibilities to spend time in the dormitories outside the prescribed visiting hours" (Kehler 1990, p. 48). The legal regulations forbade foreigners to remain in the country after the termination of the work contract or the conclusion of their education. Marriages were not possible, for the most part; furthermore, barriers would be placed in the way of any efforts to establish residence. Hence, foreigners were also prohibited from establishing businesses or opening restaurants.

The situation for Afro-Germans in the GDR was such that they had fewer possibilities to stay in contact with their black parent than did Afro-Germans in the FRG. And, due to restrictions on travel, they found themselves basically robbed of the chance of someday getting to know African relatives or at least the land of their African origin. The prescribed ghettoization of the foreign population also meant a greater isolation of black Germans, who, even more than in small West German cities, had to grow up without contact with other black people and could hardly establish connections with other ethnic/cultural populations that could have cushioned and shared certain experiences of difference and discrimination.

With regard to racism in everyday life, in comparison to the FRG, differences could be noted only in that state sanctions made racism against people with black skin and/or of African descent rather more indirect and subtle than open and raw (cf. Sithebe Nombuso, in: Hügel et al, eds., 1992). On the one hand, there was officially institutionalized solidarity with the freedom movements of oppressed peoples; at the same time, putting into practice the ideas of international solidarity on the level of everyday dealings was prevented. Racism was denied a priori as non-existent, since it essentially contradicted the constitution of a socialist society; therefore, it could hardly be officially aired. The Afro-German, Udoka Ogbue, from Dresden, reports that black Germans were not wanted in occupations that were considered representative in the GDR. For example, they were forbidden to work as attorneys or stewardesses, and it was seen as politically risky to allow them to major in similar subjects as their foreign parents.

In the meantime the face of the former GDR has come to resemble that of the former FRG. The wall between the two German states has fallen, yet estrangement between the people has remained, for the time being. Most Afro-Germans have German passports, speak the German language with no accent, and feel at home in Germany despite their experiences of exclusion. Few have reason to fear for their right of residence;

nevertheless, because of their skin color, they are threatened, just like immigrants and refugees, with verbal and physical attacks.

Black Germans and Their Organizations

Most notably black Germans starkly confront(ed) the white population of the new and old German states with the racist structures of their society. The analysis of their situation demonstrates that "anti-foreigner feelings" or "xenophobia" are expressions that irrelevantly and inappropriately describe the political and social climate in the FRG as a multi-ethnic and multi-cultural society: Basically black Germans are born and raised in Germany, many speak the German language exclusively and have never lived in another country. Just as many immigrants, who are still viewed as "foreigners" or "guest workers," black Germans are not living temporarily in this country. Furthermore, black Germans have not come to stay; they have always been here.

When, in the mid-1980s, German women of African descent came together and first documented their history and presence in German society across generations with the book *Showing Our Colors*, this was the first step toward the founding of the "Black German Initiative," (ISD) in Berlin, and the group "Afro-German Women" (ADEFRA), in Munich. Since 1986 other black German groups in West and East Germany have come into existence, some as regional sub-groups of ISD and ADEFRA. Further, both organizations have since directed themselves toward black people/women, respectively, in Germany, incorporating them as well. ISD's brochure introducing the organization says, in part:

Our definition is not restricted to skin color, but includes all minorities affected by racism. With terms such as "black Germans" and "Afro-Germans" as expression of our "multi-cultural" background we are defining ourselves instead of being defined. To meet each other, to have exchange and to share was and is for many a new experience. What we have most in common is isolation, the feeling of being enclosed in primarily white social relations, without support of a black community. Of course, we are also very diverse, through our socialization, our characters, our ages, our interests, through our experiences in family and occupation, as hetero- and homosexual women and men and in our relations to the non-European part of our heritage.

The magazine *afro look,* until 1995 a publication of ISD, now taken over by an independent editorial group, publishes scholarly contributions and project proposals as well as poetry and prose from blacks in Germany and black Germans. From 1988 until 1990 there was, in addition, *Afrekete,* published by ADEFRA and other black women, with similar content focus as *afro look.*

The objective of organized collectives of black Germans is to articulate the interests and legal claims of black people in the FRG, to wage, together with progressive whites, the struggle against racism and anti-Semitism, and to intensify, beyond the borders of the FRG, networks with organizations for immigration policy and other organizations of blacks. ADEFRA, Inc. has set as its particular objective the socio-political equality of afro-German/black women, specifically through "encouragement of intercultural women's and minority studies, the dissemination and strengthening of knowledge about blacks and other ethnic minorities in Germany and their history and cultures" (Charter 1993).

Since 1989 "Black History Month" has been organized in Berlin, by ISD, in cooperation with other black groups. As in the U.S., where the tradition of "Black History Month" goes back to the initiator Carter G. Woodson, who in 1926 first inaugurated "Negro History Week," programs also take place in the FRG every year in February. Offerings include seminars, films, readings, exhibits, theater and workshops on black culture, history, and the present.

Organizations of black Germans and immigrants have begun to link their groups and activities beyond national borders. In 1990 and 1991 two conferences took place for the first time, exclusively by and for immigrant women, black German and Jewish women, and women living in exile. Since 1978 the "Intercultural Summer Institute for Black Women's Studies" has been organized every two years, with black participants from all continents. In 1991 the hosts were black German women, and the conference, lasting several weeks, took place in Bielefeld, Frankfurt/Main, and Berlin. More and more Afro-Germans devote their attention on art, scholarship, and politics to detailed research and focus on their social and cultural history. The younger movement of black Germans, which began only about ten years ago to organize into collectives, is in the process of making themselves heard in the German and international public.

References

Brentjes, B., "Der erste afrikanische Student in Halle," in: Brentjes, B. (ed.) *Der Beitrag der Völker Afrikas zur Weltkultur*. Halle/Saale 1977.

Eyferth, K., U. Brandt, W. Hawel. *Farbige Kinder in Deutsch-*

land—Die Situation der Mischlingskinder und die Aufgaben ihrer Eingliederung. Munich 1960.

Frankenstein, L. *Soldatenkinder. Uneheliche Kinder von ausländischen Soldaten mit besonderer Berücksichtigung der Mischlinge.* Geneva 1953.

Hügel, I., Ch. Lange, M. Ayim et al (eds.). *Entfernte Verbindungen. Rassismus, Antisemitismus, Klassenunterdrückung.* Berlin 1992.

Kehler, J. "Die Lebenssituation der Migrantin in der ehemaligen DDR," in *Beiträge zur feministischen Theorie und Praxis,* no. 29, 1990.

Kirchner, W. "Eine anthropologische Studie an Mulattenkindern unter besonderer Berücksichtigung der sozialen Verhältnisse." Dissertation, Berlin 1952.

Kraft, M. and R. Shamim Ashraf-Khan. *Schwarze Frauen der Welt. Europa und Migration.* Berlin 1994.

Lester, R. *Trivialneger—Das Bild des Schwarzen im westdeutschen Illustriertenroman.* Stuttgart 1982.

Opitz (Ayim), M., Katharina Oguntoye, D. Schultz (eds). *Showing Our Colors: Afro-German Women Speak Out* (A. Adams, transl.). Amherst, UMassP, 1991.

Paeffgen, M. *Das Bild Schwarz-Afrikas in der öffentlichen Meinung der BRD 1949-1972.* Munich 1976.

Pommerin, R. *Sterilisierung der Rheinlandbastarde—Das Schicksal einer farbigen Minderheit 1918-1937.* Düsseldorf 1979.

Rogers, J.A. *Sex and Race. Negro-Caucasian Mixing in All Ages and All Lands.* St. Petersburg, FL 1952.

Theye, T. "Wir und die Wilden. Einblicke in eine kannibalistische Beziehung." Hamburg 1985.

"Wir wollen nicht glauben, sondern schauen. Zur Geschichte der ethnographischen Fotografie im deutschsprachigen Raum im 19. Jahrhundert." In: T. Theye (ed) *Der geraubte Schatten.* Munich 1989.

soul sister

saying goodbye
to someone
who is already gone
forever

moments of remembering and lapses of memory
remain
alive in movement
it's up to us

i think and i say
my personal truth

AUDRE LORDE
lived
a healthy oppositional black lesbian
life
in a sick society
on a dying planet
she died after 58 years
an ordinary death
diagnosis: cancer

her impact lives on
in her works
our visions
carry the experience
of her words

memories

1984 black german women
together with AUDRE LORDE conceived the term
afro-german
for we had many names
that were not our own
for we knew no names
by which we wanted to be called

racism remains
the pale face of a sickness
that privately and publicly eats away at us

today

we mourn the death of a great black poet
a sister and friend and comrade in struggle
her impact lives on
in her works
our visions
carry the experience
of her words

1992
for Beth and Jonathan

(Translation by Tina Campt; from *blues in schwarz weiss*)

brothers in arms sisters of the sword

territorial wars
are begun
by white men most of the time
true liberation wars
are mainly
won by black women

the most dangerous weapons are those
of sisters and brothers
the most cruel wars
are fought amongst themselves
in their own crises

hypocrisy and smiles
behind hands in front of mouths
envy
a nod of the head
a kiss
left and right on the cheek
embraces
hollow and heartless

words and jokes
icy with cutting voice
truth and myth prejudice accusation
braced and with sharp
tongue
roaring and soundless
mood
noise and paralyzing
silence

claim and character assassination
totally open and merciless
onward to the decapitation
deed and dead.

the executioners eat the last meal
eating is followed by forgetting
the distorted face of destiny
is history in the end

the underprivileged
know truth the best
because they have experienced it
day and night of their suffering
it's the brothers fighting most of the wars
it's the sisters forging the sharpest swords

(Translation by Ekpenyong Ani; from *nachtgesang*)

*from someone who is still alive to someone who has already died
a poem in memory of Martin Luther King*

the time thereafter

that one day it will be different
better
is what you dreamt, brother
black as midnight blood-red green
like the trees
soon to vanish
  —the true colors
  perhaps only children paint
  in their mother's wombs
  maybe—-

  i too have a dream, brother
  of people who one day
  are no longer born screaming
  but laughing
  laughing
  in colors of the rainbow

i carry my dream
behind
my raised first
against death and for the time thereafter
because
words are hardly useful, brother
they call it freedom of speech
also demonstrations and protest-marches
they need

for their democracy
and go on and go on and
      go on

they have preserved your dream
preserved and sold it, brother
post-cards and posters
three lines in a history book
"I Have A Dream"
a complete novel

they have
turned it into history
white as the salt of tears
and where I live
they would say "got over it," brother

i carry my dream
behind
my raised fist
in colors of pepper
and beginning really small
finally begin
with my sister
and my friend holding hands
with my brothers and
if it need be
also all alone
—so that finally change
must come!

i have a dream
of people who are no longer born screaming
and a vision

of me lying with peaceful eyes
and a hole in my head

AMEN – A LUTA CONTINUA

1987
for Linton and John

(Translation by May Ayim/Ekpenyong Ani; from *blues in schwarz weiss*)

Blues in Black and White: May Ayim (1960-1996)
by Silke Mertins

In full concentration she dug with one hand through her papers on the table of the InterCity train. In the other hand she held a book, her book, the first one by her and for her only: *blues in schwarz weiss*, poems by May Ayim. The green cloth cover felt good. She had already selected the verses she would read this evening to start off the program on racism. "exotic...to see things so darkly." But where were those notes for the talk that went with it? Should she read a love poem, too? Hmm, Love, thought May. And Love troubles. I wonder where he is? "In a few moments we will be arriving at Hanover station," announced the loudspeaker. Oh, God! Changing trains? And where to now? Hurriedly she searched for her connection, laughing about her lack of sense of direction in time and space. Papers and books got shoved together, stuffed into her bag; get off the train, onto the other one. Hopefully someone would be picking her up.

Many came that evening to hear what May Ayim had to say about Afro-German history, racism, and the "German U-noty," as she called the reunification. Her name had become a symbol, her readings and talks in great demand for programs of this sort.

Eyes alert, May gazed out over the audience. Most were white Germans. There in the back sat the skeptics. Their looks were saying: How can a distinctively beautiful, and so talented and capable woman like you have anything to complain about? We all have our little burdens to bear, one too fat, another abused, a third of lower social class. Personally, even I would be happy not to belong to these too German Germans.

In the front sat those who would hang on her every word. They wanted to be told how hard life had been for her, anxious to hear of childhood experiences, instances of discrimination, and the exposition of mechanisms of oppression from a living example. May's glance moved farther. It also met many open faces. Many had already bought her book and were leafing through it. Then, finally, two black women came in. May smiled, they both nodded to her: Sisters.

May knew what was expected of her at programs or interviews. It wasn't the universally human, the love poems or verses on everyday life that were asked for; of interest only were her blackness, the search for identity, and her work on Afro-German history. May could by now recite her sentences by heart: "I barely survived my childhood," she would smile into the audience. Or: "I ate soap to become white like my brother." And "My father used to come by my foster family's house only every couple of years, like a black Santa Claus who scared me."

The West German Radio journalist Bettina Böttinger, who had invited May to her broadcast "b.trifft" six months before May's death, proclaimed, of all May's poems, the love poem "nachtgesang" [night song] the best, in her opinion. The young poet beamed; she wanted to be recognized as a poet and not reduced to victim-verses. Many in the audience held their breath as she began to read "nachtgesang" in a melodious voice, painted words in the air with her hands, boring her gaze into the camera, as though she were alone speaking to her great love, "(...) i no longer kiss my way/down your body/through your navel/into your dreams/ (...)i no longer dream/in lonely hours/your face into time/your shadow is only a cold figure/"–her great disappointment. "Whoever got to know her felt her strength," wrote Bettina Böttinger in a eulogy to May. "A strength that in the end just wasn't enough."

People who were close to her had seen "b.trifft" not only with pride but also with concern. The sentences, articulated without any throat-clearing hesitance, sounded fit for print, in spite of the camera. Even still, this was not really May. The introverted woman, otherwise ever conscious of not revealing too much of herself, always had to force herself to bring her recollections and feelings into the open for the sake of the political message. Speaking before an audience "is my therapy," she said. But this time her bow was stretched too tight. In the high-strung state hardly discernible to anyone who didn't know her were the signs of beginning psychosis that would soon afterward bring her into psychiatric care, and from which she would never recover. On August 9, 1996, May jumped from the 13th floor of a high-rise in Berlin-Kreuzberg.

Often, as a child, she had wished not to wake up again and would hide razor blades under her pillow. The fear of life, the desire for death, were bad, but they belong to the past, said the message of the adult and politically active May. What remained, however, was fearlessness in the face of death.

The anger, the weakness, the injury of the abandoned little girl and later the youngster tormented by her foster parents were no longer recognizable in May, when she would report on her traumatic childhood from hindsight. Without bitterness she would speak about her German mother who shunted her off to an orphanage, her white foster parents who tormented her with strictness and beatings, about her blackness that she internalized, her Germanness always questioned by others. The family that took her in apparently didn't know any better and treated her so harshly out of love, she would explain. Her birth mother obviously hadn't been able to cope. And about her Ghanaian father—whom she had to call "Uncle Emmanuel"—there was never a word of reproach from her. May, the understanding one. No anger and no indictment of those who had abandoned her and who wanted to "make her white," so that she wouldn't have to "look on the dark side" of things. A few months before her death May wondered in the poem "what does a life do to die": How many "soul wounds does a heart need for the plunge to stillness"?

Almost not at all

"The day I was born a lot of stories of my life came into the world," May wrote in the book *Farbe bekennen,* which she co-edited. For the first of these stories the poet uses only a few harsh words: "the man made/the woman have a child/the woman made the child/live in a home[…]." When a white couple took her from a Hamburg orphanage, the 2-year-old could neither stand up, talk, nor eat solid food. They gave the toddler their family name: Opitz. Since, as a "pure-blooded halfbreed"—the term still used by the foster parents today—she was going to stand out anyway "like a polka-dot dog," the deportment of little Brigitte Sylvia Gertrud, nicknamed May, would have to be exemplary. By being strict the foster family wanted to make a model child out of the daughter of a (in their opinion) wayward woman and a Ghanaian medical student, to give the lie to all "racial prejudices."

Uneasily May thought back on her childhood. "There certainly was enough fear. Probably fear of the outside world. Or fear of being closed in. Fear of breaking into pieces from beatings and scoldings and of not being able to find yourself again." Her father would have liked to take her to Ghana to a childless sister but was not permitted to leave with her. As an African he had no rights to his out-of-wedlock child.

The strait-laced atmosphere of her home threatened to suffocate her. One evening, when she came home too late, the family-powderkeg exploded: May, unwilling to go; foster parents refuting to this day that they put her out. At 19 she was on her own. "The break was final," May would write. But in fact she did not make a complete break. For years she agonized over why her foster parents dismissed as after-effects of an early-childhood trauma her tough fight against racism, her success and increasing importance in the "black community." With clumsy explanations they disparaged May's activism, even while she was still alive, as a pathological need to over-come her color and Afro-German identity. Even in the face of documentation, they refused any responsibility, insisting that injury in the orphanage was irreversible and the absence of someone for May to relate to in her first two years had left a void in the behavioral programming of her interbrain: Because of pure self-absorption she was still single; her esteemed best friend, Audre Lorde—the renowned Afro-American poet—to whom she even wanted to establish a monument, was a lesbian, they added spitefully. And, besides, they loved May in spite of her bizarre behavior. The foster parents are unable to find any mistakes of their own.

In *Farbe bekennen*, 1986, May would speak openly for the first time about her loveless upbringing in the foster family; parents hit the ceiling: she was not to be allowed to publish anything like this under the name Opitz. May would do it any-way, the German legal system not allowing her to change her last name to that of her African father. Only years later would she take on "Ayim" as a pen-name.

Contact with the family was never completely severed. She would often go to the home of her beloved grandmother, to important family celebrations, and would speak regularly with her foster father. May had by no means crossed out her Muen-ster past, even though she may have buried it for periods. Per-haps, as one of her friends muses, that's why she worked so hard at building her own close, intimate friendships. A group of people with whom one can look forward to bringing in the new year, celebrating birthdays, holidays; spending vacations together; who are always there when there is anything to cele-brate or to mourn. Nevertheless, many of May's closest friends met each other only at her funeral. On her last Christmas she called "home" and got her foster father on the phone. "Does anyone else want to speak to May?" he asked into the holiday family gathering. No one wanted to.

Fatherland

"My fatherland is Ghana/my mother tongue is German/my homeland, I carry in my shoes," May wrote. She rejected categories with an almost orthodox conviction. As co-founder of the "Initiative of Black Germans" she would want to make one thing clear, first and foremost, to the blood-and-soil-oriented republic: You can take your concept of a "decay-gray" Germany, of a homogeneous, monocultural national state and throw it in the garbage dump of history. I am here, I'm black and German, German, German. I love sauerbraten with red cabbage and homemade dumplings.

May's first visit to her father, who was by now employed as a professor of medicine in Nairobi, Kenya, did not lay the groundwork for a close father-daughter relationship. Finding hardly anything to say to each other, they were still strangers: too many missed opportunities, unanswered questions and unvoiced accusations would stand between the two of them. His existence would be important for May, putting a definite face to her search for traces; but she would not glorify him. After the trip she candidly told about the difficulties in her attempts to approach her father, the chasms that opened up, her need for him to show an interest in her personally and recognition for her work. She got along much better with her father's two sons, and over time made real friends with her stepmother.

Not until years later did May decide to go to Ghana, her father's homeland. Her first impression: loud, hot, foreign. And here, also, the question "Where do you come from?" although minus the piece so often added in Germany: "When are you going back?" The Ghanaians are darker, she did not speak their language, did not know their culture, was called "white woman." She had to deal with the fact that she did not belong there either. She would have liked to blend in, to be for once one among many of the same. Whether by accident or fate, her grandfather found out that his granddaughter was in Ghana. An entire village celebrated her as a "returning daughter."

Back in Germany she began to call herself "Ghanaian-German," subordinating her black German identity to her preferred African heritage. "May related to her African roots with dignity, not exaggerated nor as a caricature of the stereotype that Europeans have about Africans," says Zimbabwean writer Tsitsi Dangarembga, then living in Berlin.

However, not Ghana, but rather South Africa, was the country where May felt most comfortable and where she could imagine living for an extended period. Not only because her great love came from that nation, but also because she "didn't stand out at all in South Africa," recalls May's friend who traveled there with her. Blackness has many shades in South Africa; the less ethnically bound and strongly politicized urban "black community" closely approximated May's needs and ideas about life. But staying in Berlin, where she had been living since 1984, allowed her to have the best of both worlds. She suffered no yearning for far-away places, but rather was essentially a woman rooted firmly in her country, who enjoyed being in Berlin skimming the borders between worlds.

Mother Tongue

May's mother tongue was not Mother's tongue, because her mother did not speak to her. In the beginning was no word. Even later she sought in vain for contact with the woman who brought her into the world. Nevertheless, words would become her passion. If May felt at home anywhere, it was in her mother tongue. She snuggled in its folds, sharpened them to word-weapons, to hit "the bull's eye" with a formulation, took it apart, put it back together anew, contorted and disfigured it or played around with its letters: "the ones with the hard edges/called themselves consonants/the ones/that pull open the mouth/claimed the name of vowels."

The German language became her connection to the outside world, the creative outlet and center of her artistic expression. No essay, no academic work, no project was as important to her as her first poetry collection *Blues in Black and White*.

Of all things, the language in which she was hurt the most would be both point and line of escape. She would not be dominated by the idiom of "nigger kisses" and of "you-are-nothing-you-can-do-nothing," but rather would appropriate it. She most liked to let the words flow onto paper at night, digging for hours for a suitable wording. May enjoyed being alone, could even smile without an interlocutor once she hit upon a satirical formulation that was just the way she wanted it. With the lines: "then every four years/we'd march/to elections/and choose without choice our top/chump" from the poem "Oktoberfest," it's easy to imagine her arrogant grin.

No one else, her friends recall, was so good at casual wordplay as May, joking around in Westphalian Low German and parental "lecturing"—I've told you a thousand times not to fidget so much, take your finger out of your nose, don't be a smart-alec." And whoever dared to hint at a complaint that May's noodles were too heavy: "There are other people who would be happy for any little meal, not to mention the poor children in Africa," she could instruct with a stern face before bursting out laughing seconds later. The collective German forefinger of "Now my little friend," or, sometimes "Missy," "no backtalk" or "Do I have to raise my voice again" reappears in the poem "zehntausendmal" [ten thousand times].

But what was served up to May in speech-therapy training, which she started in 1987 in Berlin, she found totally distasteful. A year after finishing her university studies in education, a practical occupation was now needed to support the starving artist. Once again the German language was the focal point. Like writing poetry in her mother tongue, the work of the speech therapist operates in the sphere of the German language. May looked forward to working with words, language, and children. The enthusiasm did not hold for long. "Subservience and assimilation" are expected from speech therapist trainees. Terms such as "negro" or "Hottentotism" are used without flinching. Immigrants are not among the trainees, nor do the teaching materials consider the fact that not all children are learning German as their mother tongue. As so often in the past, she was the only black training participant. May's suggestion that teaching and practice materials be reviewed for racist and sexist content was initially rejected with the remark that the meanings of words were irrelevant for speech therapy. You were to pronounce whatever was put before you.

The school administration had not figured on May's contribution to the training program. The revolt, including a strike and petitions, had long been brewing. It concerned the rigid curriculum and the authoritarian teaching methods. Even though May did not generally fraternize with the others, and often worked by herself, still, "when things got right down to it, she was out in front," recalls one of her fellow-students of those troubled times. "She had natural authority," knew exactly what she was capable of, and understood "how to get at just the right tone." "You just couldn't ignore" May's personality. In the end May's final project was accepted, in fact, with the mark of "very good." But it was still "my topic," she would recall with disappointment.

My Homeland, I Carry in My Shoes

Who are you? Where do you come from? When are you leaving? May was sick and tired of the incessant questions concerning which pigeon-hole she belonged in, the insistence on explaining herself. The idea that, because of her skin color, she was supposed to give the minutest accounting of her identity, preferably with family tree and detailed percentages of identification with the Ghanaian, the German, the Black—May found unacceptable. Of course, she would never have snapped at anyone who was interested in learning about her background; that would not have been her style. Rather, she preferred to settle in the cosmopolitan Berlin melting pot where an Afro-German did not stick out. Different from Regensburg, where May attended university, the big city offered her protection through anonymity and diversity.

"click-clack/decapitated/capitalized/capital" May made fun of the big-city airs of the strutting metropolis. It was the seedy spots, the morbid charm, and the stubborn mentality of the city's west side before reunification that appealed to her. Everybody, from the native denizens, to the beatniks and crackpots, to the newcomers—they all perched on the same Berlin island. As the crumbling Wall stirred up nationalism, the freedom of Difference was over. Violence against minorities would overshadow the much-celebrated Return. With sharp words May followed the German "U-not-y." What she was experiencing was "autumn in germany" and "i dread the winter."

Despite its "the-capital-is-capital" airs, May liked living in Berlin anyway. She loved her bright, cheerful apartment, liked her district, Schöneberg, enjoyed moving among the various subcultures. Little here reminded her of the Westphalian narrowness of her childhood or the provincialism of her university days in Regensburg. In addition to growing megalomania and construction sites, the emerging capital could also offer a bit of May's vision of the future: an existence for the most diverse groups, backgrounds, and colors, taken for granted; a co-existence with "distant ties."

May could picture Berlin as a good base. Perhaps, for a

while, she might have gone to South Africa, maybe to Ghana, most probably first to the U.S.A., where, two days after her death, she was offered a guest lectureship in Minnesota. Her "homeland" she had carried in her shoes. Surely the writer would have returned at some point to Berlin anyway. Because of the mother tongue.

Nightsong

Over and over again May would make up her mind: The next time he comes, I'm not going to wait any longer. I'm not sharing him anymore with another woman. I'm not going to cry over him. But the images of shared laughter, of gazes without words and discussions rich in words could not simply vanish. The tingling came when she heard his voice. Many were waiting for May to finally face her. But for May it had to be the very one whom she could not—entirely—have. Yearning and love troubles generated breathtakingly beautiful poems, but also opened old wounds. To have to compete with a white woman, of all people, for a black man, was a bitter pill for May. Didn't she have much more in common with him? Wasn't it true that a lot of explanations were unnecessary between them? What did the other one have that he couldn't find with her?

The fact that May at some point began to accept the existence of the other in the life of the lover, and the humiliation of the love triangle, stunned some of her confidantes. For one friend looking back on it, it was as though May couldn't bring herself to assume a right to have someone all to herself. As though she was not entitled to a whole person and his undivided love. Perhaps her feelings were just too overpowering, the conviction that he was the one man of her life. Perhaps she was able to surrender to her emotions without holding back for the very reason that she knew she could not have him. For May avoided closeness. She could only become deeply involved in relationships that would also deeply hurt her.

Touching the Pain Behind My Laughter

"I'm terribly nosey," admits one of May's friends, "but I didn't dare ask her about certain things." The certain things were not any particular things, but precisely those things that May did not want to talk about. She could erect walls and construct taboos that seemed indestructible. Any attempt to touch them would have been overstepping boundaries. "If we were having a confidential conversation, she could soon pull back into her shell," as though she had permitted the intimacy by accident. She would tell one friend that a person important to her had hurt her; the other friend she would tell who the person was. This fragmentation was typical for May. She distributed the risk of being disappointed. As well as she herself could listen to others, she intensely wished to prevent anyone knowing too much about her. In the poem "schwester" [sister] May wrote: "why do you pierce me/with your eyes/why do you want to understand everything/touch/the pain/behind my laugh-ter/feel/the weariness/in my eyes/count the furrows on my forehead/examine the scars under my skin (...)."

May did not do this out of arrogance. She was scrupulous-ly careful. "Unapproachable," she seemed to some. Never would she lose control, draw attention, be loud or unfair. "She was so human that it was almost unhuman," says one of her fel-low-students. Personal criticism of a friend would have to be pulled out of her. She did not want to burn her bridges with anyone and, when in doubt, would rather pull back.

Anyone traveling with May or organizing a program could give free vent to their thirst for confrontation. May was right there; she would manage to save the situation from getting out of hand. Always friendly, always seeking a balance. "You speak German so well," said a fellow-passenger intending to compliment May and her friend. "Can't you see that you're disturbing us?" retorted the friend. "For a visitor you sure are arrogant," came the reply. Then May, the mediator, took it up. "You did understand. So just lighten up."

Politically she would never side-step an issue. Privately, conflicts were not her style. With friendliness and laughter she would work around unpleasantness. Her motto: You don't bother me, I won't bother you. May was trusted by many. What a person told her would not go any further. Neither gossip nor clique-business excited her. She kept her circles apart, getting together usually in twos or threes, sharing only in bits.

Brothers in Arms, Sisters of the Sword

Even instructors and fellow-students benefited from May without her being able to ask for anything in return. Racism was still a non-word that belonged to the period of National Socialism, when she began her research. "There is no racism in Germany of today," May's professor in Regensburg would say in rejecting her Education thesis topic. She looked for a willing advisor in Berlin. Her research, the first on black history in Germany, became the basis of the book *Farbe bekennen. Afro-deutsche Frauen auf den Spuren ihrer Geschichte* [Showing Our Colors: Afro-German Women Speak Out]. This pioneering work was later to be published in English and became known across national boundaries. In the years that followed May would take part in conferences and black festivals in the whole world, was invited to give lectures and to be interviewed, and her poems were translated into English and Portuguese. Only through May, wrote the African-American activist Ana Sisnett, did she realize that white people could not be named European-Americans. "Because that denies the presence of immigrants, refugees, and black people" on the European continent. She became a part of an international community that was shocked and incredulous when it learned of the young poet's death.

Whether as a student, an adjunct teacher or later as academic counselor, May was nearly always the only black. "White stress and black nerves" she calls the "stress factor racism" in an essay. Rejecting discriminatory terms usually isn't enough. It is "expected" of black people "that they patiently and diplomatically explain why. And sometimes, on top of that, they even have to put up with the accusation of being too 'sensitive.'"

"May was always a bit of a learning process," acknowledges her dissertation advisor Helmut Essinger, who taught anti-racist education at the Free University. "She directed me." With May, it goes without saying that this happened in a friendly manner. Without rancor she would bring "linguistic derailments" to Essinger's attention. He was able to take the criticism well. She, for her part, did not make an issue about the academic advising to which she was in fact entitled, as, again, her knowledge about systemic racism was much broader and thorough than her teacher's. She did not go around denouncing the fact that, in multicultural Berlin, white men held the positions that were concerned with intercultural learning. Now and then, in an abstract way, she would make the observation that she was the only black person teaching at the school.

May chose her allies carefully. She was dependable when it came to executing a project. Without her, say many Afro-Germans openly, they would not have found their way to the "Black Community," or not until much later. Without her research, the principal sections of *Farbe bekennen*, the "Initiative Schwarze Deutsche"—the initial spark of a black movement in the FRG—would not have developed so quickly.

With success came envy. From other blacks, it hurt her the most. After publication of the co-edited book, *Entfernte Verbindungen*, and especially when her first volume of verse appeared in bookshops, the evil tongues started wagging: May was being glamorized into a "star," was commercializing herself, or her success was going to her head. Some just could not manage to give her credit for her hard-earned recognition. In the poem "brothers in arms, sisters of the sword" she attempted to work out the painful experience of all-too-human meanness: "hypocrisy and smiles/behind hands in front of mouths/envy/a nod of the head/a kiss/left and right on the cheek/embraces/hollow and heartless (...)"

What Shall the Last Words Be

Like a madwoman May worked in the last weeks before her breakdown. Eating, drinking, sleeping? That could wait. Day and night she was busy almost exclusively with the organization of the annual "Black History Month" in Berlin. A euphoric high-flight that dropped her into a deep hole. Her friends felt helpless. What should they do? Commit her to psychotherapy, of which May herself said there was no place free of racism? "The psychosis was like a volcano," recalls one friend. Everything suddenly broke out from her, the screams, too. There was only in-patient treatment. Her friends looked in on her daily. Her father came but was also unable to give his daughter any support. Because she reported earlier vision problems she was moved to neurology and examined for multiple sclerosis. For unexplained reasons the medications for her psychosis, neuroleptica, were abruptly discontinued. When the doctors informed her of the MS diagnosis, she had no psychological support. Cognizant of the presence of an incurable disease they released the psychically ill May.

Seven months of soul-torture, one suicide attempt with pills, another psychiatric stay—May's will to live had been broken. Nothing could brake her fall into the depths. She feared that she would not be able to find the way back to her personality, she said to the handful of friends who cared for her: Her life's thread was broken; "what should the last words be," she wrote in the poem from that period "departure."

Much too much came together, when she decided, on August 9, 1996, to make a sure end to her life by jumping out of the 13th floor: The serious illness, memories, an endless sadness, an unfulfilled love, a depressing German present. It couldn't be possible, says a friend, for a young black person to be released from psychiatry and sent home alone. How is it possible that they can't find out how many blacks are actually being treated in German psychiatric facilities, how many commit suicide—the basis for establishing any system of assistance? "A whole population could destroy itself without anyone knowing."

Some things have been put in motion since then. May's death shook the "Black Community" in Germany and encouraged it not to individualize the psychic problems of blacks, not to leave them alone with breakdowns. A society that allows all manner of abuse, denigration, and ignorance, and maybe doesn't find the murder of minorities exactly acceptable—for many, it is the last straw. It re-moves their Self. The burden of bearing and wanting to change all of this was too much for May: This, too, is a message of her leap into the depths. What shall be the last words?

May Ayim leaves behind her courage, her strength, and her vision; two volumes of poetry, her research and many people who must come to grips with her decision.

P.S. I thank May Ayim's friends who gave time and energy to speak with me. The title and section headings for this text have been borrowed from May's poems in *blues in schwarz weiss* and *nachtgesang.*

Silke Mertins, born in 1965, is an editor of *Financial Times Deutschland* in Berlin. Her book, *Zwischentöne: Jüdische Frauenstimmen aus Israel* [Nuances: Voices of Jewish Women in Israel] was published in 1992 by Orlanda Frauenverlag.

preparing for the emergency

the inner agitation
sits between diaphragm
and imagination eating
a banana
it digests
a reliable recipe
for pretty nervousness

start with thorough relaxing
then get upset unnecessarily
then
don't inhale
before you've
reached the limit

the inner agitation
smacks
quietly in time

when all of that
doesn't help
comes contemplating
everything
we have always
wanted to forget
and should

misunderstandings excuses
conflicts
thoughtlessness self-deception
remorse

lies accusations
spitefulness
and so on and so on
and so on

a good memory
is an advantage for this
but needn't be
common
remembrance
is usually sufficient

even in refractory cases
eventually secret
doubts arise

followed however
right away by why and how come
after all the central
interposed question

how on earth do you
imagine this
to continue
and end

or...?
(or...is very popular
and important at this point!)
or has
it all come to an end already
and you just
didn't say so
or

dared not say so

now
the agitation is
complete
contemplation and doubts
are gone
no question

the emergency
may set in

5-3-1995

(Translation by Ekpenyong Ani; from *nachtgesang*)

in the face of death

the outside
turns
inward

the periphery
loses
its tragedy

breath
murmurs
deep and dark
ebbing and flowing

in the rhythm of the moon

momentary glances
backward and forward
gestures and expressions
disappear
in remaining traces

gestures and expressions
disappear

in remaining traces
reminders

under the skin
pulsate
immortal
words

in the face of death is

life

for Audre and Hedwig

(Translation by Tina Campt; *from nachtgesang*)

nightsong

i no longer wait
for the better times
midnight blue sky above us
silver stars upon it
hand in hand with you
along the river
trees right and left
desire in their branches
hope in my heart

      i straighten up my room
      i light a candle
      i paint a poem

i no longer kiss my way
down your body
through your navel
into your dreams
my love in your mouth
your fire in my lap
pearls of sweat on my skin

      i dress myself warmly
      i paint my lips red
      i talk to the flowers

i no longer listen
for a sign from you
take out your letters
look at your pictures
conversation with you

till midnight
visions between us
children smiling at us

        i open the window wide
        i tie my shoes tight
        i get my hat

i no longer dream
in lonely hours
your face into time
your shadow is only
a cold figure

        i pack the memories up
        i blow the candle out
        i open the door

i no longer wait
for the better times
i go out into the street
scent of flowers on my skin
umbrella in my hand
along the river
midnight blue sky above me
silver stars upon it
trees
left and right
desire in their branches
hope in my heart

i love you
i wait no longer

1992

(Translation by Tina Campt; from *blues in schwarz weiss*)

departure

what should the last words be
fare-well see you again
sometime somewhere?
what should the last deeds be
a last letter a phone call
a soft song?
what should the last wish be
forgive me
forget me not
I love you?
what should the last thought be
thank you?
thank you

(Translation by Dagmar Schultz; from *nachtgesang*)

afterword

alone
i would never have found
my way here
of that i am certain

many have accompanied me
some have even carried me

through love rage and courage
i have grown
can move around freely

show weakness
tears

laughter
can joke around

unlearn mistakes
ignorance

i can
recognize and
cope with
competition and envy

not always
but more often than not

share pain and happiness
without all those

who loyally stand by me
stood by me

on my own
i would never have made it all the way
let alone found my way
here
to you all to me

for critique and patience
optimism and trouble

for everyone
that ever stands by me
stood by me

a million thanks
and a
big

kiss!

1994

(Translation by Ekpenyong Ani; from *blues in schwarz weiss*)

May Ayim: Curriculum Vitae

5/3/1960	birth in Hamburg, Germany, daughter of Ursula Andler and Emmanuel Ayim
1960-61	institutionalization in a children's home
1962-79	growing up with the foster family Opitz
1966-70	elementary school, St. Michael, Muenster
1970-79	episcopal comprehensive school, "Friedensschule," Muenster, graduation with "Abitur"
1978	training and qualification as an assistant nurse
Fall 1979	enrollment at the teacher's college, Muenster, with majors in German and social studies
1979	trip to Israel and Egypt
Fall 1980	new choice of majors: psychology and education at the University of Regensburg
1980	stay at the Kibbutz Gesher Haziv in Israel
1981/82	two-month internship at the National Family Welfare Center in Nairobi, Kenya
1984/85	stay in Ghana
1986	graduation in education, University of Regensburg; thesis: *Afro-Germans: Their Cultural and Social History on the Background of Societal Change*
1987	publication of the thesis in the book, *Showing our Colors: Afro-German Women Speak Out:* edited by Katharina Oguntoye, May Opitz and Dagmar Schultz
1986	co-founder of Initiative of Black Germans and Black People in Germany (ISD)
1986	three-month work and study trip to Ghana with the International Youth Community Service
1986/87	associate lecturer at the Free University of Berlin, interdisciplinary research project on

"changing female identities"

1987	enrollment at the School for Logopaedia, Berlin, for training as a speech therapist
1988	reading at the 2nd International Cross-Cultural Black Women's Studies Summer Institute, New York, USA
1988	trip to Senegal
1989	co-founder of "LiteraturFrauen e.V.," society for the promotion of literature by women; member of the board
1989/90	trip to Brazil
1990	state examination in speech therapy
1990	speech therapist at a special learning school (Heilpädagogisches Therapeutikum Berlin) for mentally disabled children; thesis: *Ethnocentrism and Sexism in Speech Therapy*
1991	study and research trip to South Africa (Johannesburg, Cape Town, Durban) in co-operation with the faculty of education, Free University of Berlin
Nov. 1991	talk at the conference, Education in Transition. Education and Education Planning for a Post-Apartheid Society in South Africa, Berlin, Nov. 19-24
1991	membership at the Association of German Writers
1991-95	freelancing as a speech therapist
1992-95	lectureships at the Alice Salomon School for Social Work and Social Pedagogy; at the Free University of Berlin in the department of education and the institute for sociology; at the Technical University in the department of social pedagogy, focusing on women's studies
1992	publication of the translation *Showing our*

	Colors: Afro-German Women Speak Out in the USA and UK
1992	adoption of the name Ayim as a pen-name
1992	enrollment at the Free University of Berlin in the department of education; Ph.D. topic: *Ethnocentrism and Racism in Therapy*
July 1992	reading at the conference, CELAFI (Celebrating African Identity) of the Canadian Artists Network: Black Artists in Action, Toronto, July 7-12 (with other authors, i.e. Grace Nichols, Lisa Jones, Danny Laferriére, Dionne Brand)
Oct. 1992	"My Pen is My Sword: Racism and Resistance in Germany," talk at the conference, African Women Living in Europe, Akina Mama Wa Afrika, London, Oct. 30-31
1993	publication of the book, *Entfernte Verbindungen (Distant Ties: Racism, Anti-Semitism, Class Oppression)*, co-editor and author
3/23/1993	reading at the festival of the 11th International Book Fair of Radical Black & Third World Books, London, March 21-27 (with other authors, i.e. June Jordan, Paule Marshall, Linton Kwesi Johnson, Margaret Busby, Sonia Sanchez)
1993	invitation to the European Round Table on Human Rights and Cultural Politics in a Changing Europe: The Right to Participate in Cultural Life, Council of Europe and UNESCO, Helsinki, Apr. 30-May 2
1/28/1994	"Writings from the Edge; Writings from Inside," talk at the conference, Testaments: Writers at the Crossroads, ZABALAZA, London, Jan. 28-31 (with other authors, i.e. Ronald

Segal, Pitika Ntuli, John La Rose, Merle Collins)

1994	meeting with Maryse Condé; moderator of her reading in Berlin, interview February 25
1994	study trip to Cuba
5/13/1994	"Racism and Resistance in United Germany," talk at the conference, Xenophobia in Germany: National and Cultural Identities after Unification, Minneapolis, Minnesota, May 11-14 (with other authors, i.e. Dan Diner, Yüksel Pazakaya); further talks at Carleton College, Northfield, Minnesota; Earlham College, Richmond, Indiana; several schools in Chicago, Illinois
July 1994	reading at the Round Table Programme on Cultural Equity, AKWAABA, Brussels, July 29-31
Oct. 1994	reading at the international symposium, Racisms and Feminisms in preparation for the World Conference on Women, ARGE Viennese Ethnologists and the minister for women, Oct. 29-30
Dec. 1994	talk at PANAFEST (Pan-African Historical Theatre Festival), Accra, Ghana, Dec. 9-18
1995	employment as a student counselor at the Alice Salomon School for Social Work and Social Pedagogy, Berlin
Apr. 1995	reading at Mega Music Festival in Johannesburg, South Africa, April 10-21; talks at schools in Johannesburg and at the University of Transkei, Umtata
Sept. 1995	publication of a collection of poetry: *blues in schwarz weiss (blues in black and white)*
10/11/1995	interview with Deutsche Welle TV

10/12/1995	reading and interview for the WDR TV program, Literature in the Roemer during the Frankfurt Book Fair
Oct. 1995	invitation to Africa 95: A Season Celebrating the Arts of Africa, presentation of the book *Daughters of Africa*, Nottingham, UK
1/5/1996	guest at the talk-show "b.trifft" with Bettina Böttinger (broadcasting date: Jan. 19)
1/8/1996	admission into the psychiatric ward of Auguste Viktoria Hospital, Berlin
Apr. 1996	discharge from the clinic
Apr. 1996	assistance at Orlanda publishing house (until end of May)
June 1996	second hospitalization at Urban hospital, Berlin (until mid-July)
July 1996	resumption of work at the Alice Salomon School
8/9/1996	suicide

(Translated by Ekpenyong Ani)

Bibliography of English Language Publications

PRIMARY LITERATURE

Books and academic publications (as author or editor)

Opitz (Ayim), May/Oguntoye, Katharina/Schultz, Dagmar (eds.): *Showing our Colors: Afro-German Women Speak Out;* Boston (The University of Massachusetts Press, Amherst) 1992.

Opitz (Ayim), May/Oguntoye, Katharina/Schultz, Dagmar (eds.): *Showing our Colors: Afro-German Women Speak Out;* London (Open Letters) 1992. (no longer available)

Contributions in books

Articles/Essays
"Departure." In: Busby, Margaret (ed.): *Daughters of Africa: An International Anthology of Words and Writings by Women of African Descent from the Ancient Egypt to the Present,* London (Jonathan Cape) 1992, pp. 932-935.

Poems
"Afro-German I," "Afro-German II." In: Busby, Margaret (ed.): *Daughters of Africa.* London (Jonathan Cape) 1992, pp. 935-937. (see Articles/Essays)

"Rhythm and Soul," "Nightsong," "The Time Thereafter," "Afro-German," "Borderless and Brazen," "In Exile," "HIV Positive," "Afro-German II," "Blues in Black and White." In:

SuAndi (ed.): *AKWAABA (Pan European Women's Network for Intercultural Action an Exchange)*. *May Ayim, SuAndi, Jamila, Rose Tuelo Brock* (poetry in three languages: English, German, Dutch), Pankhurst Press, Manchester 1995, pp. 9-45 (with short biography in three languages).

Contributions in Magazines/Newspapers

Poems
"Afro-German I." In: Conditions collective (eds.): *Conditions: fourteen* (international focus II); Baltimore, Maryland 1987, p. 5.

"Afro-German I," "Afro-German II." In: *The Black Scholar: Journal of Black Studies and Research*, Volume 19, No. 4/5, July/Aug.-Sept./Oct. 1988; Oakland, California 1988, p. 42.

"Afro-German: Two Poems by May Opitz" ("Afro-German I," "Afro-German II"). In: *The Bridge: Newsletter of the Military Counseling Network* (bilingual Newspaper German/English), No. 2, June 1989; Sindelfingen 1989, p. 6 (with a short biography). (see Reports/Essays/Reviews/Interviews/Conversations

"Blues in Black and White." In: *The Minnesota Daily*, 5/18/1994, p. 7 (see Secondary Literature)

Reports/Essays/Reviews/Interviews/Conversations
"Speak your mind. A talk with May Opitz and John Amoateng..." In: *AWA-FINNABA. An African literary cultural journal*, No.9, March 1987; Berlin 1987, pp. 52-56

"Searching for my father. Excerpts from a conversation

between Eleonore Wiedenroth and May Opitz (Ayim)." In: *The Bridge. Newsletter of the Military Counseling Network*, No. 2, June 1987, p. 7

"The Way We Deal With Our Fear" (conversation with May Ayim and Eleonore Wiedenroth). Ibid.

"Walking Targets. Afro-German Women Speak Out" (conversation with May Ayim and Eleonore Wiedenroth). In: *Ms. Magazine,* Volume III, No.6; New York 1993, p. 93.

Lectures and Readings at Events, Conventions and Conferences

Lectures (available in written form)

"Transculturalism in education II." In: *Education in transition* (education and education planning for a post-apartheid-society in South Africa). Report of the Berlin conference, Nov. 19-24, 1991 (convention reader); Berlin 1992, pp. 197-201.

"My Pen is My Sword: Racism and Resistance in Germany" (summary of the lecture). In: *African Women in Europe. Report of a conference convened by Akina Mama Wa Afrika* (conference reader, Oct. 30-31, 1992); London 1993, p. 25/26.

Lectures/Talks (in oral form)

Toronto, July 7-12, 1992: *CELAFI. Celebrating African Identity: The Third International NCA Conference* (brochure and program): Literary Readings (promotion of a reading with May Ayim); Toronto 1992, pp. 67-74 (short biography, p. 68)
London, March 21-27, 1993: "Bigotry, Racism, Nazism and Fascism in Europe" (promotion of talk and reading). In: 11th International Book Fair of Radical Black and Third World

Books (brochure/program with short biography, p. 23); London 1993

Utrecht, May 21-23, 1993: International MEP-festival, reading

London, Jan. 28-31, 1994: ZABALAZA, *Testaments; Writers at the Crossroads*, reading "Writings from the Edge; Writings from Inside"

Minneapolis, Minn., May 10, 1994: University of Minnesota, Leighton Hall: 1993-1994 Light Lectureship for Literature presented by the German and Russian Department, talk "Racism and Resistance in United Germany"

Minneapolis, Minn., May 13, 1994: University of Minnesota, Center of European Studies *Xenophobia in Germany: National and Cultural Identities after Unification*, May 11-14, 1994: "Racism and Resistance in United Germany" (promotion of the talk in the convention program). Further talks at Carleton College, Northfield, Minnesota; Earlham College, Richmond, Indiana; several schools in Chicago, Illinois

Brussels, July 30, 1994: AKWAABA (Pan European Women's Network for Intercultural Action an Exchange). Round Table Programme (of the conference, from July 29-30): "Poetry Performance" (May Ayim and others)

Accra, Dec. 9-18, 1994: *Pan-African Historical Theatre Festival* (PANAFEST 94); Cape Coast/Accra, Ghana 1994: Colloquium (diploma for participants)

Johannesburg, Apr. 10-21, 1995: *Mega Music Festival*: reading; talks at schools in Johannesburg and at the University of Transkei, Umtata

Publications/Translations in Other Languages

"Sem fronteiras e orgulhosa. Um poema contra a pretensa unidade da alemanha." In: *Sim da vida. Boletim Especial do CEAP*, 10/93; Rio de Janeiro 1993

SECONDARY LITERATURE

On Showing our Colo(u)rs

"Showing our Colors: Afro-German Women Speak Out." In: *The Black Scholar*, Volume 22, No. 3; Oakland, California, pp. 83-84

"Showing our Colors: Afro-German Women Speak Out." In: *WLW Journal* 15:3, Fall 1992; USA

"Showing our Colours: Afro-German Women Speak Out." In: *Wasafiri. Focus on writing in Britain*, No. 17, Spring 1993; London 1993, pp.67-68

"Showing our Colours: Afro-German Women Speak Out." In: *African Woman. Bi-annual Development Journal*, Issue 7, June-Nov. 1993; pp. 52-53

"On the Edge of he Margin. Showing our Colors: Afro-German Women Speak Out." In: *The Women's Review of Books*, Volume X, No. 2, Nov. 1992; pp.6-7

On Other Topics

"A Question of Unity: May Ayim searches for recognition in a reunified Germany," by Michael Sampson. In: *The Carletonian*, 5/13/1994; Minneapolis, Minnesota 1994, pp.5-6

"Author: African-Germans subject to neo-Nazis' wrath." In: *The Minnesota Daily*, 5/17/1994; Minnesota 1994, pp. 3-5

---

* Black servant of Santa Claus, who beats bad kids